T0305768

MICROECONOMICS
with SPREADSHEETS

MICROECONOMICS
with SPREADSHEETS

Suren Basov

Deakin University, Australia

World Scientific

EW JERSEY · LONDON · SINGAPORE · BEIJING · SHANGHAI · HONG KONG · TAIPEI · CHENNAI · TOKYO

Published by

World Scientific Publishing Co. Pte. Ltd.

5 Toh Tuck Link, Singapore 596224

USA office: 27 Warren Street, Suite 401-402, Hackensack, NJ 07601

UK office: 57 Shelton Street, Covent Garden, London WC2H 9HE

Library of Congress Cataloging-in-Publication Data
Names: Basov, Suren, author.
Title: Microeconomics with spreadsheets / Suren Basov (Deakin University, Australia).
Description: New Jersey : World Scientific, 2016.
Identifiers: LCCN 2016032487 | ISBN 9789813143951 (hc : alk. paper)
Subjects: LCSH: Microeconomics.
Classification: LCC HB172 .B367 2016 | DDC 338.50285/554--dc23
LC record available at https://lccn.loc.gov/2016032487

British Library Cataloguing-in-Publication Data
A catalogue record for this book is available from the British Library.

Desk Editors: Suraj Kumar/Philly Lim

Typeset by Stallion Press
Email: enquiries@stallionpress.com

Printed in Singapore

Preface

Microeconomics studies the choices made by individuals under conditions of scarcity of resources and time and the interaction between different decision makers. Scarcity forces economic actors to choose one opportunity among many, which leads to the *opportunity costs*. Opportunity cost is the value of the best forgone alternative. For example, by deciding to enroll to a graduate programme, you forgo the opportunity to hold a job. The salary you might have earned on such a job is the opportunity cost of your education, which should be counted together with the cost of textbooks and tuition costs to give the total cost of your education.

In choosing the amounts of goods and services that individuals consume, a crucial question is how much of a particular good should a financially constrained individual consume. The principle of marginalism states that the goods should be consumed in such quantities as to leave individual indifferent between spending her last dollar on any of the goods. Indeed, if she prefers to spend her last dollar on apples, she would be better off by buying more apples.

The principles of marginalism and opportunity costs are the central tenets of the economic method of thinking. Formally, they are captured by the following assumption of rational behavior: *individuals seek to maximize a well-defined objective function subject to some constraints*. For example, consumers form their demands by maximizing utility, subject to budget constraints, firms maximize profits, a mechanism designer maximizes some private or public objective subject to the incentive compatibility and individual rationality constraints, etc.

Some recent developments called into question the very utility maximization paradigm and drove a wedge between preferences and utilities. Such models are known as bounded rationality models. It is not a place to discuss these models in this course. It suffices to say that most techniques you will learn in this course will still be relevant in studying bounded rationality models. Moreover, since such models are analytically less tractable than the standard models, knowledge of numerical tools, such as Excel, becomes even more important.

This book brings together a comprehensive and rigorous presentation of microeconomic theory suitable for an advanced undergraduate course, simple Excel-based numerical tools suitable for an analysis of typical optimization problems are encountered in the course.

Due to the importance of constraint optimization technique, I devote the first part of the book to its formal exposition. I also introduce the reader to a standard Excel tool: the Solver, which is a convenient tool to analyze optimization problems. The rest of the necessary mathematics is delegated to an Appendix. The book covers the following economic topics: consumer theory, producer theory, general equilibrium, game theory, basics of industrial organization and markets, and economics of information.

The first three of those topics study situation, where individuals do not need to explicitly take into account behavior of other economic actors, i.e., they act non-strategically. The actions of different economic actors are mediated via prices. We call such interactions *market interactions*. However, most situations of economic interest are dominated by interaction of many individuals. Such interactions, known as *strategic interactions*, are dominated by a relatively small number of participants (for example, firms on an oligopolistic market). In such situations, it becomes crucial for market participants to be able to predict behavior of their opponents and respond in an appropriate way. Such situations are the subject of study of game theory. Problems in both general equilibrium and game theory lead to systems of simultaneous equations, which can also be analyzed using Solver. The sections, marked with * are more technical than the rest of the text and can be omitted by the instructor without damage to the rest of the course.

Supplementary matrials can be accessed at: http://www.worldscientific. com/worldscibooks/10.1142/10138

Author Biography

 Suren Basov graduated from Boston University with a PhD in Economics in 2001. He held academic positions in Melbourne University, La Trobe University, and a visiting position at Deakin University and published extensively in various branches of economic theory. This book is based on the lecture notes for Microeconomics class the author taught at Melbourne University and Decision Analysis with Spreadsheet class he taught at La Trobe University.

Contents

PART I

Mathematical Preliminaries

Overview

In this part, I am going to present the main mathematical tool that we will use during the course: constraint optimization. While presenting this material, I will assume that the students are familiar with calculus, matrix algebra, basic logic and set theoretic notations. However, for the reader not familiar with any of these techniques, they, together with some other techniques used in this course, are presented in the Mathematical Appendix in the last part of the book.

Chapter 1

Constraint Optimization

This chapter introduces reader to constraint optimization technique that is used through the book.

1.1 Constraint optimization with equality constraints

Often in economics, you are asked to maximize or minimize an objective function subject to some constraints. For example, consumers are assumed to maximize their utility given their budget and prices, firms often have to find an optimal way to produce a given quantity of products, which leads to minimizing cost of production taking the level of production, technology, and factor prices as given, etc. One can always turn a constraint minimization into a constraint maximization by changing the sign of the objective function. Therefore, we will formulate all results for constraint maximization problems. Ubiquity of constraint optimization problems in economics comes from the central assumption that economic agents act rationally in pursuing their self-interest. Main mathematical result that allows one to deal with the constraint optimization problems is summarized in the following theorem.

Theorem 1. *Let $f \colon X \to R$ be a real-valued function and $g \colon X \to R^m$ be a mapping, where $X \subset R^n$. Let us consider the following optimization problem:*

$$\max f(x) \tag{1.1}$$

$$\text{s.t. } g(\mathbf{x}) = \boldsymbol{\theta}. \tag{1.2}$$

Assume that the solution is achieved at x_0 and vectors $(\nabla g_1(x_0), \ldots,$ $\nabla g_m(x_0))$ are linearly independent non-degenerate constraint qualifications (NDCQ). Then

$$\frac{\partial f}{\partial x_i}(\mathbf{x}_0) = \sum_{j=1}^{m} \lambda_j \frac{\partial g_j}{\partial x_i}(\mathbf{x}_0). \tag{1.3}$$

Intuitively, if (1.3) does not hold, one can find point $x_0 + \delta x$ such that

$$g(\mathbf{x}_0 + \boldsymbol{\delta}\mathbf{x}) = \boldsymbol{0}.$$

Recall that

$$f(\mathbf{x}_0 + \boldsymbol{\delta}\mathbf{x}) - f(\mathbf{x}_0) = \nabla f(\mathbf{x}_0) \cdot \boldsymbol{\delta}\mathbf{x} + o(\|\boldsymbol{\delta}\mathbf{x}\|).$$

Therefore, for x_0 to be the optimum $\nabla f(x_0) \cdot \delta x$ should be zero. Now, note that locally the surface $g(x) = \theta$ looks like a hyperplane and $(\nabla g_1(x_0), \ldots, \nabla g_m(x_0))$ forms a basis (by NDCQ) in its orthogonal complement. Therefore,

$$\nabla f(\mathbf{x}_0) = \sum_{j=1}^{m} \lambda_j \nabla g_j(\mathbf{x}_0) \tag{1.4}$$

for some $\lambda_1, \ldots, \lambda_m$.

Proof. Note that NDCQ implies that $m \leq n$. If $m = n$, then vectors $(\nabla g_1(x_0), \ldots, \nabla g_m(x_0))$ form a basis in R^n and expansion (1.4) can be found for any vector, including $\nabla f(\mathbf{x}_0)$. Therefore, from now on, we will assume that $m < n$. NDCQ is equivalent to the statement that the Jacobian matrix J, defined by

$$J_{ij} = \frac{\partial g_j}{\partial x_i}, \tag{1.5}$$

has full rank at x_0. Therefore, it must have m independent rows. Without loss of generality, we will assume that first m rows of the Jacobian matrix, evaluated at x_0, are independent.[1] Therefore, Eq. (1.3) can be made to hold

---

[1] We can always achieve it by appropriately relabeling the variables.

for $i = \overline{1, m}$ by choosing

$$\lambda = -J_m^{-1} b, \tag{1.6}$$

where J_m is an $m \times m$ matrix formed by the first m rows of matrix J and

$$b = \left(\frac{\partial f}{\partial x_1}, \ldots, \frac{\partial f}{\partial x_m} \right). \tag{1.7}$$

To prove that Eq. (1.3) also holds for $i = \overline{m + 1, n}$ for the same choice of λ, recall that by the Implicit Function Theorem,[2] there exist a neighborhood[3] U of point x_0 and continuously differentiable functions $h_j(\cdot) : R^{n-m} \to R^m$, $j = \overline{1, m}$, such that $x_j = h_j(x_{m+1}, \ldots, x_n)$ for all $x \in U$. Moreover,

$$\nabla h_j = (J_m^{-1})^T \nabla_{n-m} g_j, \tag{1.8}$$

where ∇_{n-m} denotes vector of partial derivatives with respect to variables $(x_{m+1}, \ldots, x_n)$.

Note that x_0 delivers an unconstraint local maximum to function

$$F(x_{m+1}, \ldots, x_n)$$
$$= f((h_1(x_{m+1}, \ldots, x_n), \ldots, h_m(x_{m+1}, \ldots, x_n), x_{m+1}, \ldots, x_n)). \tag{1.9}$$

Using the first-order condition for unconstraint optimization and the chain rule, one can write the following:

$$\frac{\partial F}{\partial x_i} = \frac{\partial f}{\partial x_i} + \sum_{j=1}^{m} b_j \frac{\partial h_j}{\partial x_i} = 0. \tag{1.10}$$

Note that in matrix notation,

$$\sum_{j=1}^{m} b_j \frac{\partial h_j}{\partial x_i} = b \cdot (J_m^{-1})^T \nabla_{n-m} g = J_m^{-1} b \cdot \nabla_{n-m} g = -\sum_{j=1}^{m} \lambda_j \frac{\partial g_j}{\partial x_i}, \tag{1.11}$$

which completes the proof. $\qquad\qquad\qquad\qquad\qquad\qquad\qquad\square$

---

[2]See Mathematical Appendix in the end of the book for the formulation of the Implicit Function Theorem and other mathematical concepts used throughout the book.
[3]A neighborhood of a point is an open set containing the point.

1.2   Constraint optimization with inequality constraints

Sometimes, relevant constraints are represented by inequalities rather than equalities. For example, a consumer may be offered a menu of choices. Relevant incentive constraints, which we will discuss later in this course, will specify that she should like the item designed for her at least as much as any other item on the menu. Generalization of the above theorem for the case of inequality constraints is given by the following theorem.

Theorem 2. *Let $f: X \to R$ be a real-valued functional and $g: X \to R^m$ be a mapping, where $X \subset R^n$. Let us consider the following optimization problem:*

$$\max f(x) \tag{1.12}$$

$$\text{s.t. } g(\mathbf{x}) \leq \boldsymbol{\theta}. \tag{1.13}$$

Assume that the solution is achieved at x_0 and vectors $(\nabla g_1(x_0), \ldots, \nabla g_m(x_0))$ are linearly independent (NDCQ). Then

$$\frac{\partial f}{\partial x_i}(\mathbf{x}_0) = \sum_{j=1}^{m} \lambda_j \frac{\partial g_j}{\partial x_i}(\mathbf{x}_0), \tag{1.14}$$

$$\boldsymbol{\lambda} \geq 0, \boldsymbol{\lambda} \cdot (\mathbf{g}(\mathbf{x}) - \boldsymbol{\theta}) = 0. \tag{1.15}$$

This statement is known as the Kunh–Tucker theorem. Intuitively, the first-order conditions state that the gradient of the objective function should look in a direction in which all the constraints are increasing, since otherwise one can move in a direction that will leave the choice variable $\mathbf{x}$ within the constraint set, but increase the value of the objective. I will not give the complete proof of this theorem. However, it is quite easy to see intuitively why it is true. Indeed, if a certain constraint does not bind, i.e., $g_i(x) < \theta_i$, then it can simply be dropped, which corresponds to setting $\lambda_i = 0$. If neither constraint is binding, then vector $\lambda = 0$ and the first-order conditions reduce to those for unconstraint optimization. Therefore, one needs to have (possibly non-zero) Lagrange multipliers only for binding constraints, i.e., the constraints that hold with equality.[4] The only subtle point is the sign of the Lagrange multipliers. Let us assume that $\lambda_i < 0$.

---

[4]The corresponding Lagrange multiplier may still turn out to be zero.

This means that the objective function is increasing in the direction of decrease of $g_i(\cdot)$, keeping all other constraints at the fixed level.[5] Note that NDCQ guarantees that such a direction exists and therefore, the objective function can be increased without violating any constraints. Note also that writing constraints in a form $g(\mathbf{x}) \leq \boldsymbol{\theta}$ is without loss of generality, since constraint,

$$g_i(x) \geq \theta_i, \qquad (1.16)$$

can be always replaced by

$$-g_i(x) \geq -\theta_i. \qquad (1.17)$$

1.3 Introduction to Solver and using Solver to solve constraint optimization problems

Some constraint optimization problems are too complicated to be solved analytically. In that case, one has to restore to numerical analysis. Here, I would like to describe an Excel-based application, Solver, which is particularly well suited for the analysis of constraint optimization problems. When preparing an Excel spreadsheet to analyze a constraint optimization problem, one has to organize the data for the model. The first step is to reserve separate cells to represent each decision variable in the model. Then, create a formula in a cell corresponding to the objective function. Create a formula in a separate cell corresponding to the LHS of each constraint. It will be useful to familiarize yourself with the terminology used by the Solver. The cell representing the objective function is known as the *objective (target) cell*, the cells representing the decision variables are known as the *variable (changing) cells*, the cells representing LHS of the constraints are known as the *constraint cells*.

The main objectives you have to keep in mind when devising a spreadsheet are: *communication*, it should be easy to communicate information to others, *reliability*, correct and consistent output, *auditability*, being able to retrace the steps of generating the different outputs from the model, and

---

[5]Recall that a function increases in the direction of its gradient, decreases in the opposite direction, and stays constant in the direction orthogonal to the gradient.

modifiability, should be easy to change or enhance in order to meet dynamic user requirements.

Let us consider the following example. Suppose you need to solve ⋅

$$\max(a \ln x + b \ln y)$$
$$\text{s.t. } px + qy = w. \tag{1.18}$$

To find a solution, form a Lagrangian:

$$L = a \ln x + b \ln y - \lambda(x + y - w). \tag{1.19}$$

The first-order conditions are

$$\begin{cases} a = \lambda x, \\ b = \lambda y, \\ px + qy = w. \end{cases} \tag{1.20}$$

It is easy to see that the system possesses a unique solution

$$\begin{cases} x = \frac{wa}{(a+b)p}, \\ y = \frac{wb}{(a+b)q}, \\ \lambda = \frac{pa+qb}{w}. \end{cases} \tag{1.21}$$

Therefore, if a maximum exists, it must be achieved at point

$$(x^*, y^*) = \left(\frac{wa}{(a+b)p}, \frac{wb}{(a+b)q} \right). \tag{1.22}$$

In Mathematical Appendix in the end of the book, I present theorems that will allow you to prove the existence of the solution. You can also persuade yourself that (x^*, y^*) is indeed a solution graphically by thinking of the objective as the utility function and drawing the corresponding indifference curves, which are hyperbolas. Indeed, recall that

$$\ln x + \ln y = \ln(xy), \tag{1.23}$$

and therefore, the equation for the indifference curves is

$$xy = c, \tag{1.24}$$

where $c > 0$ is some constant.

To see how to implement the problem in Excel, open file Chapter_1.xlsx (Available at: http://www.worldscientific.com/worldscibooks/ 10.1142/10138). For the ease of communication, give a title to each sheet in your file. For now, follow sheet *Constraint Optimization*. Select some cells to be changing cells, in the example, these are cells B5 and C5. Program the value of objective to the target cell, in this case D6. Note that you have to specify particular values of parameters p, q, a, b, and w to run the program. In this example, I selected

$$a = b = p = q = 1, \ w = 10. \tag{1.25}$$

However, formula for cell D6 reads

$$D6 = B6 * \ln(B5) + C6 * \ln(C5), \tag{1.26}$$

rather than

$$D6 = \ln(B5) + \ln(C5). \tag{1.27}$$

The same applies to the other cells. For example, cell D9 contains expression for the constraint with values of p and q stored in cells B9 and C9. It is done to allow you to study easily how the solution will change if some of the parameters change. For example, if you would like to know what would happen if parameter q becomes equal to two, all you have to do is to change the value in the cell corresponding to q, rather than to change the formulae. Therefore, your spreadsheet is easily modifiable. Once you set up your cells, open the Solver.

In Excel 2010, Solver is available in the Analysis group on the Data tab. If it does not appear there, you will need to load it first. The Solver Add-in is a Microsoft Excel Add-in program that is available when you install Microsoft Office or Excel. To use it in Excel, however, you need to load it first. To achieve it, first click the File tab, and then click Options. Click Add-Ins, and then in the Manage box, select Excel Add-ins, and click Go. In the Add-Ins available box, select the Solver Add-in check box, and then click OK.[6] After you load the Solver Add-in, the Solver command is available in the Analysis group on the Data tab. If you are using another version of Excel, consult the Excel help, which can be reached by pressing F1 on your keyboard.

Once you have Solver, open it and in the *Set Objective* box, enter a cell reference or name for the objective cell. In our example, it is cell D6.

---

[6]If Solver Add-in is not listed in the Add-ins available box, click Browse to locate the Add-in, if you get prompted that the Solver Add-in is not currently installed on your computer, click Yes to install it.

Remember, *the objective cell must contain a formula*. We are trying to maximize our objective function, therefore, from the next row in the dialog box, select *Max*. In the by *Changing Variable Cells* box, enter a name for each decision variable cell range. In our case, the changing cells are B5 and C5. In general, the changing cells need not be adjacent. If this is the case, separate the non-adjacent references with commas. You can specify up to 200 variable cells. Finally, we have to specify the constraints. To do this, in the *Subject to the Constraints* box, enter all the constraints for the problem, following the procedure outlined below. First, in the *Solver Parameters* dialog box, click *Add* and in the *Cell Reference* box, enter the name of the cell range for which you want to constrain the value. In our case, it is cell D9. Then click one of the relationships <=, which stands for ≤, =, or >=, which stands for ≥, that you want between the referenced cell and the constraint.[7] Then type a number, a cell reference or name, or a formula. For reasons of modifiability and auditability, it is preferable to put a cell reference that can contain a number or a formula. In our case, it is cell E9, which contains the value to w. Finally, to accept the constraint and add another, click *Add* and to accept the constraint and return to the Solver Parameters dialog box, click OK. You can change or delete an existing constraint by going to the *Solver Parameters* dialog box and clicking the constraint that you want to change or delete. Then click *Change* and then make your changes, or click *Delete*. Based on the nature of your problem, choose one of the solving methods, used by the Solver. For a general smooth problem (like the one in this example), choose *Generalized Reduced Gradient* (*GRG*). For linear problems, choose *LP Simplex*. For non-smooth problems, use *Evolutionary*. For all problems encountered in this course, you will need to use GRG. Finally, click *Solve* and *Keep Solver Solution*.

If you apply the procedure to the example above with parameters given by (Eq. (1.25)), you will obtain solution $x = y = 5$, which coincides with one produced by formula (Eq. (1.22)).

1.3.1 *Some pitfalls of numerical optimization*

In our example, you had to maximize a strictly concave objective on a convex set. In such a problem, the target function has at most one local

---

[7]You can also constrain the variable to be binary or integer. But we will not need these options for the applications considered in this book.

maximum, which is also a global one and Excel has no problem in finding it. In practice often, optimization problems are not convex. In that case, the problem can possess several local maxima, but only one of them will be global. Consider a function,

$$y = 2x^3 + 3x^2 - 12x + 6.$$

Suppose you would like to find the maximal value of y subject to $x \in [-3, 4]$. First, let us find the derivative, y'. Easy calculation shows that it is given by

$$y' = 6x^2 + 6x - 12. \tag{1.28}$$

To find candidates for local maxima and minima, solve $y' = 0$, i.e.,

$$6x^2 + 6x - 12 = 0. \tag{1.29}$$

One obtains $x_1 = 1, x_2 = -2$. The second derivative, y'', is given by

$$y'' = 12x + 6. \tag{1.30}$$

Note that

$$y''(-2) = -18 < 0, \tag{1.31}$$
$$y''(1) = 18 > 0, \tag{1.32}$$

therefore, -2 is a local maximum with a value

$$y(-2) = 2 * (-2)^3 + 3 * (-2)^2 - 12 * (-2) + 6 = 26, \tag{1.33}$$

and 1 is a local minimum with a value

$$y(1) = 2 * 1^3 + 3 * 1^2 - 12 * 1 + 6 = -1. \tag{1.34}$$

However, note that the value of function at $x = 4$ is 134, therefore y achieves its global maximum at point $x = 4$.

To see how to implement the problem in Excel, open file Chapter_1. xlsx (Available at: http://www.worldscientific.com/worldscibooks/10.1142/ 10138), sheet *Local versus Global*. You will see that the set up for the problem is replicated twice: in rows 5–10 and 14–19. The difference is that variable cell B5 was initialized by putting their value -3, while cell B14 was initialized by putting their value 3. If you do this and run the Solver, in the first case, you will come up with candidate solution $x = -2$ and in the second with $x = 4$, the correct solution. In fact, you will come up with candidate solution $x = -2$ for any initial value of $x \in [-3, 1)$. The reason for this is that Excel will move at the direction of increase of the function and stop when it reaches the local maximum or the boundary of allowed set of values. Since $y'(x) > 0$ for $x \in [-3, -2)$ and $y'(x) < 0$ for $x \in (-2, -1)$, it will converge to -2 for any initial condition in this region. On the other hand, if initial value of $x \in (1, 4]$, it will converge to $x = 4$.

The lesson of the above considerations is that before running Excel or any other software, you should first establish that the problem has a solution. It is also useful to analyze whether there exists unique local maximum, which in that case will also turn out to be the global maximum. If it is the case, you can run the program. Otherwise, it will be useful to try to localize the approximate position of the global maximum analytically and choose the initial condition close to it. If it proves to be too difficult, it is useful to try to choose different initial values for the variables cells and see whether the solution is affected.

1.4 Envelope theorem for constraint optimization and the economic meaning of Lagrange multipliers*

So far, we have learned how to solve constraint optimization problems. In applications, economists often want to not only solve the problem for some particular values of the parameters, but also analyze how the value of the objective changes for the small changes in the parameter value. The answer to this question is provided by the following theorem.

Theorem 3. *Let $f(x, y)$ and $g_1(x, y), \ldots, g_m(x, y)$ be continuously differentiable, NDCQ holds. Let $x(y)$ solve*

$$\max_{x \in X} f(x, y)$$

$$\text{s.t. } g_j(x, y) \leq 0.$$

Define

$$V(y) = \max_{x \in X} f(x, y)$$

$$\text{s.t. } g_j(x, y) \leq 0.$$

Then

$$V'(y) = \frac{\partial L(x(y), y)}{\partial y},$$

$$L = f(x, y) + \sum_{j=1}^{m} \lambda_j g_j(x, y).$$

1.5 Problems

(1) Using Lagrange method, solve the following constraint optimization problem:

$$\max(x + y)$$
$$\text{s.t. } x^2 + y^2 = 1. \tag{1.35}$$

(2) Consider the following constraint optimization problem:

$$\max(x + y)$$
$$\text{s.t. } x^2 + a\sqrt{xy} + y^2 = 1, \tag{1.36}$$

where parameter $a \in [0, 1]$. Set up an Excel spreadsheet for the problem and solve it for each $a \in \{0, 0.2, 0.4, 0.6, 0.8, 1\}$. Compare the solution for $a = 0$ with the one you obtained in Problem 1.[8]

---

[8]When developing a spreadsheet or writing a computer code to deal with a complicated problem, it is always useful to be able to find a simple version of the problem that you can solve by hand to compare with the solution obtained by the program. Even working programs contain bugs.

Bibliographic notes

Theoretical material covered in this chapter is rather standard. A reader who wishes to obtain a more thorough knowledge of mathematical concepts and techniques relevant for economic analysis can consult numerous texts on mathematical economics. A good text is de la Fuente (2000), which introduces the reader to such topics as metric spaces, differential calculus, comparative statics, convexity, static optimization, dynamical systems and dynamic optimization, which enable her to follow the standard first-year theory sequence in micro and macroeconomics. A good reference for basics of Excel is Ragsdale (2001).

References

A. de la Fuente, *Mathematical Methods and Models for Economists*, Cambridge University Press, Cambridge, UK, 2000.

C. Ragsdale, *Spreadsheet Modelling and Decision Analysis,* South-Western College Publishing, Mason, OH, USA, 2001.

PART II
Market Interactions

Overview

In this part of the book, we will consider *market interactions*. This means that we assume that economic agents, when making decisions, do not directly take into account behavior of others. Rather, this behavior is summarized in the vector of prices, including prices of the goods and factor prices, which each economic agent takes as given. Actors in the market place can be divided into two broad categories: consumers and producers. Consumers choose their consumption baskets to maximize their utilities and producers choose production plans to maximize profits. Of course, the same agent may play both roles. If this is the case, we assume that the agent's action in one role has no non-pecuniary effect of her choice in the other role. We will also assume that the agents neglect the effect of their actions on prices. Strictly speaking, the last assumption requires one to have an infinite number of economic agents, but in practice, the assumption provides a good enough approximation for large but finite number of economic agents.

We start this part with the study of the consumer theory and theory of demand. Then we move to the producer theory and theory of supply. Finally, we bring them together in the general equilibrium theory. It is useful to have the following diagram in mind when discussing the market interactions:

Chapter 2

The Consumer Theory

In this chapter, we are going to discuss the process of formation of a consumer's demand. Demand of a consumer for good i is a function defined on the prices of all available goods that specifies how much of good i will the consumer like to purchase given the realization of prices. We assume that consumers form their demands rationally, i.e., they result from a deliberation that proceeds as follows. With each bundle of goods, the consumer associates a number that measures her satisfaction from the consumption of the bundle. This number is known as the utility of the bundle. The consumer selects the bundle that maximizes her utility. In doing so, she faces a budget constraint. Often, it is reasonable to assume that amount of goods cannot be negative, in which case consumer also faces non-negativity constraints.

It is possible to link the notion of utility with a more fundamental notion of preferences. We will discuss this later in this chapter. For now, let us proceed with the formal statement of the consumer's problem.

2.1 The formal statement of the consumer's problem

Formally, the consumer's problem is as follows:

$$\max u(x)$$
$$\text{s.t. } p \cdot x \le w, \ x \ge 0. \tag{2.1}$$

Here, $u(\cdot)$ is the consumer's utility function, $w > 0$ is her wealth, $p \in R^n_+$ is the vector of prices and $x \in R^n_+$ is the vector of goods. The solution of

this problem, when it exists, is known as consumer's Marshallian demand.[1]
It depends on the prices and the wealth.

Suppose there are L goods in the economy and consider the set:

$$B(p, w) = \{x \in R^L | p \cdot x \leq w_i, \ x \geq 0\}. \tag{2.2}$$

This set is known as the budget set. Its outer boundary is known as budget
hyperplane. Observe the budget set is closed (it contains its boundary) and
bounded, provided all prices are strictly positive, i.e., it is compact.

Suppose $L = 2$. The set

$$\{x \in R_+^2 | u(x) = \text{const}\}, \tag{2.3}$$

is known as the indifference curve.[2] Geometrically, consumer's demand can
be found as a tangency point between the budget line and an indifference
curve.[3]

Let us now use analytical techniques we learned in Chapter 1 to write
the first-order conditions for the consumer problem. For simplicity, assume
for now that all goods are consumed in positive amount, so we can drop
the non-negativity constraints. Then the consumer's problem is

$$\max u(x) \\ \text{s.t. } p \cdot x \leq w. \tag{2.4}$$

The Lagrangian for this problem is

$$L = u(x) - \lambda(p \cdot x - w), \tag{2.5}$$

which leads to the following first-order conditions:

$$p_i = \lambda \frac{\partial U}{\partial x_i}, \lambda \geq 0, p \cdot x \leq w, \lambda(p \cdot x - w) = 0. \tag{2.6}$$

Assume $\lambda \neq 0$, which implies that the individual uses her entire wealth to
purchase goods $(p \cdot x = w)$.[4] Then we can write

$$\frac{p_i}{p_j} = \frac{\partial U/\partial x_i}{\partial U/\partial x_j}. \tag{2.7}$$

---

[1] A sufficient condition for the existence is that $u(\cdot)$ is continuous and all the prices
are strictly positive.
[2] For $L > 2$, it is known as indifference surface.
[3] Or budget hyperplane and indifference surface if $L > 2$.
[4] We will see in subsequent text that λ is the marginal utility of income.

The RHS of this equation is known as the marginal rate of substitution (MRS).

To figure out the geometric meaning of MRS, assume $L = 2$ at a totally differentiate condition,

$$U(x_1, x_2) = \text{const},\tag{2.8}$$

to obtain

$$\frac{\partial U}{\partial x_i} dx_i + \frac{\partial U}{\partial x_j} dx_j = 0,\tag{2.9}$$

to obtain

$$\frac{dx_j}{dx_i} = -\frac{\partial U/\partial x_i}{\partial U/\partial x_j}.$$

Therefore, MRS is the slope of the indifference curve.

To figure out the economic meaning of MRS let the consumer consume at point (x, y). Consider another point $(x + \Delta x,\ y - \Delta y)$ on the same indifference curve. Define the average rate of substitution (ARS) by,

$$\text{ARS} = \frac{\Delta y}{\Delta x}.$$

ARS measures how much of good x you have to get to compensate for the loss of a unit of good y. MRS is the limit of ARS as Δx and Δy become small. These observations allow us to discuss on the roles of prices in the light of Eq. (2.7). Note that in a market economy all consumers act as price takers and face the same prices. Equation (2.7) implies that prices equate marginal rates of substitution among consumers for any pair of goods. If at the margin Ann value an orange at two bananas so will Bob, Catherine, and any other consumer in the economy.[5] Therefore, it is impossible for Ann and Bob, or anybody else, to exchange oranges for bananas among themselves in such a way as to make both better off. Equation (2.7) leads to *an allocative efficiency* of price mechanism.

2.2 Preferences and utility*

In the previous section, we assumed that a consumer can assign a numerical index to each bundle of goods in such a way that more preferred items were

---

[5] As long as they consume positive amounts of bananas and oranges.

always assigned higher numerical indices. We called such an index *utility function*. In this Section, we are going to ask: what assumptions should preferences satisfy to make such an assignment possible. Let us start with some definitions.

Definition 1. A binary relation $\succeq$ on set R_+^m is said to be complete if for any $x, y \in R_+^m$ either $x \succeq y$ or $y \succeq x$. It is said to be transitive if for any $x, y, z \in R_+^m$ if $x \succeq y$ and $y \succeq z$ then $x \succeq z$.

In the definition above, we assumed that $x, y, z, \ldots$ are elements of R_+^m. This assumption is not crucial, completeness and transitivity can be defined on any set. However, since in all applications choice variables will always be vectors of real numbers, we will not pursue a more general approach. Preference of a consumer between bundles of goods is simply a binary relation, where $x \succeq y$ means that the consumer prefers bundle x to bundle y.

Definition 2. Preference relation is called rational if it is represented by complete and transitive binary relation.

Rationality means that the consumer is able to compare any two bundles. The consumer is allowed to be indifferent, but cannot say that she does not know which bundle is better. Transitivity means that there are no cycles in preferences. Intuitively, this requirement seems reasonable, since otherwise one can use the consumer as a money pump. For example, assume Bob prefers an apple to an orange, an orange to a banana, but prefers a banana to an apple, and is in possession of an orange. Ann can offer to exchange an orange for an apple for a fee, which Bob would agree, provided the fee is sufficiently small. Now, Ann can trade apple for a banana also for a sufficiently small fee. Finally, she trades the banana for an orange, and Bob is back with an orange having paid Ann three fees.

Our final definition captures the notion that preferences are representable by a utility function.

Definition 3. Preference $\succeq$ relation on R_+^m is representable by a utility function if there exists $u : R_+^m \to R$ such that

$$(x \succeq y) \Leftrightarrow (u(x) \geq u(y)). \tag{2.10}$$

What conditions should a preference relation satisfy to be representable by a utility function? First easy observation that in order to be representable by a utility function preference relation should be rational.

Lemma 4. *Any preference relation representable by a utility function is rational.*

Proof. Indeed, since $(x \succeq y) \Leftrightarrow (u(x) \geq u(y))$. Since $u(x)$ and $u(y)$ are real numbers, it is always true that either $u(x) \geq u(y)$ or $u(y) \geq u(x)$, therefore completeness holds. Note that $x \succeq y$ and $y \succeq z$ imply that $u(x) \geq u(y)$ and $u(y) \geq u(z)$. Again, since $u(x)$, $u(y)$ and $u(z)$ are real numbers, it implies that $u(x) \geq u(z)$ and therefore $x \succeq z$. $\square$

Unfortunately, rationality is not sufficient for the preferences to be representable by a utility function.

Example 5. Let $m = 2$ and let us define preference relation on R_+^2 by

$$\{x \in R_+^2 : x \succeq y\} = \{x \in R_+^2 : x_1 > y_1\} \cup \{x \in R_+^2 : x_1 = y_1, x_2 \geq y_2\}. \tag{2.11}$$

In words, given any two bundles we first compare the amount of the first good, say apples, in the bundles and if bundle x has more apples it is preferred no matter what amount of second good, say bananas, each bundle has. If they have the same number of apples, the one with more bananas is preferred. Such preferences are known as lexicographic, since bundles are ordered like words in a dictionary. The reader should convince herself that lexicographic preferences are rational. However, they cannot be represented by any utility function. Indeed, assume to the contrary that such a utility function exists. Then it will map a ray $x = a$ into an interval $[r_1^a, r_2^a]$, where $r_1^a = u(a, 0)$ and

$$r_2^a = \lim_{y \to +\infty} u(a, y). \tag{2.12}$$

The limit exists, since $u(a, \cdot)$ is increasing and bounded, for example, by $u(a+1, 0)$. Note that $r_2^a > r_1^a$ and $r_1^a > r_2^b$, provided $a > b$. Therefore, these intervals are non-empty and do not intersect. For each $a \in R_+$, choose a rational number $q^a \in [r_1^a, r_2^a]$. Such a number exists, since $r_2^a > r_1^a$ and $q^a \neq q^b$, provided $a \neq b$. Therefore, we defined an injection of R_+ into Q, the set of rational numbers. However, such an injection will imply that cardinality of R_+ is at most countable, which is known to be false.

This example shows that rationality of preferences is necessary but not sufficient for the preferences to be representable by a utility function. One needs a technical condition, called continuity.

Definition 6. Preference $\succeq$ relation on R_+^m is called continuous if the following sets are closed:

$$\{x \in R_+^2 : x \succeq y\}, \{x \in R_+^2 : y \succeq x\}. \tag{2.13}$$

To understand this definition intuitively, let us define indifference and strict preference.

Definition 7. We say that $x \sim y$ (read: x is indifferent to y) if $x \succeq y$ and $y \succeq x$. We say that $x \succ y$ (read: x is strictly preferred to y) if $x \succeq y$ and not $y \succeq x$.

Using this definition and the observation and open sets are exactly the complements of the closed sets, one can rephrase the definition of continuity of preferences requiring sets

$$\{x \in R_+^2 : x \succ y\}, \{x \in R_+^2 : y \succ x\}, \tag{2.14}$$

to be open in R_+^2. The last requirement is equivalent to saying that if a consumer strictly prefers x to y, she will also strictly prefer any bundle that is sufficiently close to x to y. It turns out that any rational continuous preference can be represented by an utility function. Moreover, the utility function can be always chosen to be continuous. The proof of the last statement is too technical and we will not provide it here.[6]

2.2.1 *Convex preferences*

In general, the indifference curve can be tangent to the budget line at several points, i.e., the consumer will have a *demand correspondence* rather than a *demand function*. However, there is an important class of preferences for which demand is a function.

Definition 8. Preference relation $\succeq$ is called *strictly convex* if for $\forall x_1, x_2$ and $\forall \theta \in [0, 1]$:

$$\theta x_1 + (1 - \theta)x_2 \succ x_1 \quad \text{and} \quad \theta x_1 + (1 - \theta)x_2 \succ x_1. \tag{2.15}$$

---

[6]Note that the utility function representing given preferences is not unique. Indeed, if $u : R_+^m \to R$ if one such function and $\phi : R \to R$ is strictly increasing, then $v = \phi \circ u$, is also a utility function representing the same preferences.

If preferences are representable by a utility function definition (2.15) implies:

$$u(\theta x_1 + (1 - \theta)x_2) > \max(u(x_1), u(x_2)). \qquad (2.16)$$

Functions satisfying definition (2.16) are known as *strictly quasiconvex*. Geometrically, it means that the set of bundles above the indifference curve is convex. From an economic point of view, convex preferences can be interpreted as preferences for diversity. For example, one peach and one apple is preferred to both two peaches and two apples. If preferences are strictly convex, the optimal consumption bundle is unique, i.e., demand is a function.

2.3 Properties of demand

From now on, we will always assume that preferences are representable by a continuous strictly quasiconvex function, unless explicitly specified otherwise. We will also assume that all the prices are strictly positive, so the budget set is compact. Under these conditions, solution to problem (2.1) exists and is unique.

Definition 9. Fix a price vector $p \in R_{++}^L$. Then the solution of problem (2.1) defines a function from prices and wealth into consumption bundles and is known as the Marshallian demand function.

Let us study some properties of the demand.

Lemma 10 (Walras Law). *Assume that utility function is strictly increasing*[7] *in each argument. Then,*

$$\sum_{i=1}^{L} p_i x_i(p, w) = w. \qquad (2.17)$$

This law says that the consumer spends all her budget, i.e., does not leave money on the table.

---

[7]In fact, as it is evident from the proof, a weaker condition, known as local non-satiation is sufficient: it requires that for any bundle $x \in R_+^L$ and any real number $\varepsilon > 0$, there exists y such that $y \succ x$ and distance between x and y is less than ε.

Proof. Since demand should satisfy the budget constraint, one can write:

$$\sum_{i=1}^{L} p_i x_i(p, w) \leq w. \tag{2.18}$$

Assume that contrary to the assertion of the lemma,

$$\sum_{i=1}^{L} p_i x_i(p, w) < w. \tag{2.19}$$

Consider a bundle $x_i' = x_i(p, w) + \varepsilon * \mathbf{1}$, where $\mathbf{1} = (1, 1, \ldots, 1)$ and $\varepsilon > 0$. Note that for sufficiently small ε,

$$\sum_{i=1}^{L} p_i x_i' < w, \tag{2.20}$$

therefore bundle x' is affordable and since it contains more of every good than $x(p, w)$, it is preferred to $x(p, w)$, which contradicts to the assumption that the latter is the optimal bundle. □

Our second property effectively states if you start to measure money is cents rather than dollars nothing will change.

Lemma 11. *Consumer demand is homogenous of degree zero in prices and wealth, i.e., for any $\lambda > 0$*

$$x(\lambda p, \lambda w) = x(p, w).$$

Proof. Inspection of problem (2.1) shows that if one multiplies both prices and wealth by the same constant $\lambda > 0$, the problem will not change, since prices and wealth do not enter the utility function and the common factor $\lambda > 0$ will cancel from the budget constraint. □

Note that Walras Law and homogeneity of degree zero survive aggregation, i.e., the value of the aggregate demand equals the total wealth and the aggregate demand is homogenous of degree zero, where the aggregate demand is defined as the sum of individual demand of the consumers.

$$x(p; w_1, \ldots, w_n) = \sum_{i=1}^{n} x_i(p, w_i).$$

It turns out that any set of functions satisfying these two properties can be realized as an aggregate demand of some economy populated by rational consumers. However, utility maximization imposes some more subtle conditions on the individual demands. The best known of these conditions is, the *Weak Axiom of Revealed Preferences (WARP)*.

Axiom 12 (WARP). *If*

$$p' \cdot x(p, w) \leq w' \tag{2.21}$$

and

$$x(p, w) \neq x(p', w'), \tag{2.22}$$

then

$$p \cdot x(p', w') > w. \tag{2.23}$$

In words: if the old demand $x(p, w)$ is still feasible under (p', w') but not chosen, it must be that $x(p', w')$ is preferred to it. Therefore, for $x(p, w)$ to be chosen under (p, w), the bundle $x(p', w')$ should not be feasible. This is in principle a testable restriction. Unfortunately, to test it one needs to observe an individual's demand and it is lost in aggregation.

Depending on how demand for a good responds to changes in income and prices the goods can be classified into three categories.

Definition 13. A good is called normal if demand for it increases in wealth.

The richer you are, the more of a normal good you will buy. Almost all known goods fall into this category.

Definition 14. A good is called inferior if demand for it decreases in wealth.

The richer you are, less of the inferior good you buy. The reason is that now you substitute away from it to more expensive goods. The example might be potato. You consume a lot of it if you are poor, and substitute away from it, say to meat, as you grow rich.

Definition 15. A good is called Giffen if demand for it increases with its price.

We will see later that Giffen goods are necessarily inferior. As price rise leaves you poorer you may want to substitute it for more expensive goods.

2.4 Marshallian demands for some commonly used utility functions

Let us find Marshallian demands for some commonly used utility functions.

Example 16. Let an individual's utility function be given by:

$$u(x,y) = x^\alpha y^{1-\alpha}, \qquad (2.24)$$

for some $\alpha \in (0,1)$. This utility function is known as *Cobb–Douglas* utility. Let $p > 0$ and $q > 0$ be the prices of goods x and y and $w > 0$ the individual's wealth.

$$\max x^\alpha y^{1-\alpha}, \qquad (2.25)$$
$$\text{s.t. } px + qy \leq w, \ x \geq 0, \ y \geq 0. \qquad (2.26)$$

First, note that $x = 0$ or $y = 0$ can never be optimal. Indeed $u(0,y) = u(x,0) = 0$, while spending half of the wealth on each good, for example, will provide the individual with a positive utility. Therefore, non-negativity constraints do not bind and can be omitted. Form the Lagrangian

$$L = x^\alpha y^{1-\alpha} - \lambda(px + qy - w). \qquad (2.27)$$

The first-order necessary conditions are:

$$\frac{\partial L}{\partial x} = \alpha \left(\frac{y}{x}\right)^{1-\alpha} - \lambda p = 0, \qquad (2.28)$$

$$\frac{\partial L}{\partial y} = (1-\alpha) \left(\frac{x}{y}\right)^{\alpha} - \lambda q = 0, \qquad (2.29)$$

$$\lambda(px + qy - w) = 0, \qquad (2.30)$$

$$\lambda \geq 0, \quad px + qy \leq w. \qquad (2.31)$$

First, note that if $\lambda = 0$ then the first of these equations imply $y/x = 0$, while the second $x/y = 0$. Since these cannot hold simultaneously, $\lambda \neq 0$ and therefore, $px + qy = w$, i.e., the budget constraint binds (we could have guessed this without any calculations, since the utility is increasing in both goods. Therefore, it is never optimal to leave money on the table). Writing first two equations in a form,

$$\alpha \left(\frac{y}{x}\right)^{1-\alpha} = \lambda p, \qquad (2.32)$$

$$(1-\alpha) \left(\frac{x}{y}\right)^{\alpha} = \lambda q \qquad (2.33)$$

and dividing one by the other one obtains

$$\frac{\alpha y}{(1-\alpha)x} = \frac{p}{q}, \qquad (2.34)$$

or

$$y = \frac{(1-\alpha)px}{\alpha q}. \qquad (2.35)$$

Substituting it into the budget constraint, one obtains

$$px + q\frac{(1-\alpha)px}{\alpha q} = w. \qquad (2.36)$$

Cancelling q in the numerator and denominator in the second term and multiplying both sides by α

$$\alpha px + (1-\alpha)px = \alpha w, \qquad (2.37)$$

or

$$x = \frac{\alpha w}{p}. \qquad (2.38)$$

Finally, substituting it into (2.35), one obtains

$$y = \frac{(1-\alpha)w}{q}. \qquad (2.39)$$

Note that for Cobb–Douglas preferences, the income shares spent on goods x and y are constant, i.e., they do not depend on prices and wealth. Indeed,

$$s_x = \frac{px}{w} = \alpha, \qquad (2.40)$$

$$s_y = \frac{qy}{w} = 1 - \alpha. \qquad (2.41)$$

If one aggregates goods in sufficiently coarse groups (e.g., industrial products and food), then consumption shares are indeed rather stable in time, though relative prices may change. This observation led Cobb and Douglas to introduce this utility function in the first place.

Example 17. Let us assume that the utility function is given by:

$$u(x, y) = \alpha \ln x + (1 - \alpha) \ln y - \beta \exp(-x), \qquad (2.42)$$

where $\alpha \in (0, 1)$ and $\beta \geq 0$. Note that for $\beta = 0$ utility (2.42) is simply the logarithm of utility (2.24). Since logarithm is an increasing function, both utilities represent the same preferences and therefore Marshallian demand in that case is given by (2.38)–(2.39). In general case, we proceed in the same way as in Example 1. The Lagrangian is:

$$L = \alpha \ln x + (1 - \alpha) \ln y - \beta \exp(-x) - \lambda(px + qy - w), \qquad (2.43)$$

and the first-order conditions are:

$$\frac{\alpha}{x} + \beta \exp(-x) = \lambda p, \qquad (2.44)$$

$$\frac{1 - \alpha}{y} = \lambda q, \qquad (2.45)$$

$$px + qy = w. \qquad (2.46)$$

Dividing (2.44) by (2.45), and solving (2.46) for y, one obtains:

$$\left(\frac{\alpha}{x} + \beta \exp(-x) \right) (w - px) = (1 - \alpha)p. \qquad (2.47)$$

It is easy to see that for $\beta = 0$, Eq. (2.47) can be solved explicitly to obtain[8]:

$$x = \frac{\alpha w}{p}. \qquad (2.48)$$

In general, one cannot solve Eq. (2.47) explicitly, but since the LHS is strictly decreasing in x from $+\infty$ to 0 as x changes from 0 to w/p and the RHS is a positive constant, it has a unique solution. To find the solution, let us set up an Excel spreadsheet. To access the spreadsheet, open file Chapter_2.xlsx (Available at: http://www.worldscientific.com/worldscibooks/10.1142/10138), sheet Marshallian Demand. In that file, cells B5 and C5 are designated as variable cells, and coefficients α and β are in cells B6 and C6, respectively. Cell D6, the objective cell, has the formula (2.42)

---

[8]It is always useful to check that your equation gives the correct solution for the case you have already solved. In this way, you can make sure that you did not make a mistake in your calculations.

programmed into it, prices are in the cells B9 and C9 and the budget constraint is programmed into cell D9. In the example, $p = q = 1$, $w = 8$, $\alpha = 0.5$, $\beta = 0.3$. Quantities demanded, found by the Solver, are $x = 4.08$, $y = 3.92$. Again, it is always useful to run the program for the values of the parameters, for which you know the answer. If $\beta = 0$, you can explicitly calculate the quantities demanded using (2.38)–(2.39) to be $x = y = 4$. Run Solver for this parameter, values and verifies that this is indeed the case.

This example demonstrates how to calculate Marshallian demand using Excel. Once you set up the spreadsheet, you can start asking policy questions. For example, you can ask how would the demand change if the government levies sales tax at rate t on good x. All you have to do is to multiply the price of x by $(1 + t)$.

Example 18. Let an individual's utility function be given by:

$$u(x, y) = x + y. \tag{2.49}$$

Let $p > 0$ and $q > 0$, be the prices of goods x and y and $w > 0$ the individual's wealth. Goods x and y are called *perfect substitutes*. To find the individual's demand for x and y solve

$$\max(x + y), \tag{2.50}$$
$$\text{s.t. } px + qy \leq w, \ x \geq 0, \ y \geq 0. \tag{2.51}$$

There are two ways to approach this problem.

The First Approach. First, note that since the utility increases in both goods, the budget constraint holds as an equality. From the budget constraint, one can write

$$x = \frac{w - qy}{p}, \tag{2.52}$$

and since $y \geq 0$ we see that $0 \leq x \leq w/p$. For a similar reason, $0 \leq y \leq w/q$, i.e., the amount of each good is between zero and the amount that can be purchased if all the money is spent on it. Substitute (2.52) into the individual's utility to obtain:

$$\max\left(\left(1 - \frac{q}{p}\right)y + \frac{w}{p}\right). \tag{2.53}$$

If $q > p$, then the individual's utility is decreasing in y, therefore the utility is maximized at $y = 0$, if $q < p$, then the individual's utility is increasing in y, therefore the utility is maximized at $y = w/q$, if $q = p$, then the individual's utility does not depend on y, therefore the demand for y is any y between 0 and w/q. The demand for x is determined from the budget constraint. To sum up:

(1) If $q > p$: $x = w/p$, $y = 0$ (all wealth is spent on x).
(2) If $q = p$: $x \in [0, w/p]$, $y \in [0, w/q]$, $px + qy = w$ (wealth is divided arbitrary between x and y).
(3) If $q < p$: $x = 0$, $y = w/q$ (all wealth is spent on y).

The result is rather intuitive. Since goods are perfect substitutes, the individual spends all her money on the cheapest good and divides it between the goods arbitrary if their price is the same.

The Second Approach. This approach provides you with a useful demonstration how Lagrange method works when there are binding inequality constraints. When you learn a new method, it is always useful to start by applying it to a problem with a known solution to see that you understand how it works, before moving to more complicated cases. To proceed, write the Lagrangian

$$L = x + y - \lambda(px + qy - w) + \mu_1 x + \mu_2 y. \tag{2.54}$$

The first-order conditions are

$$\frac{\partial L}{\partial x} = 1 - \lambda p + \mu_1 = 0, \tag{2.55}$$

$$\frac{\partial L}{\partial y} = 1 - \lambda q + \mu_2 = 0, \tag{2.56}$$

$$px + qy \leq w, \ x \geq 0, \ y \geq 0, \tag{2.57}$$

$$\lambda \geq 0, \ \mu_1 \geq 0, \ \mu_2 \geq 0, \tag{2.58}$$

$$\lambda(px + qy - w) = 0, \mu_1 x = 0, \mu_2 y = 0. \tag{2.59}$$

First, note that $\lambda > 0$. Indeed, if $\lambda = 0$, then $\mu_1 = \mu_2 = -1$, which contradicts (2.58). Therefore, the budget constraint holds as equality. Subtracting the second of the equations from the first one obtains

$$\mu_1 - \mu_2 = \lambda(p - q). \tag{2.60}$$

Multiplying (2.60) by y

$$\mu_1 y = \lambda(p - q)y. \tag{2.61}$$

If $p < q$, then the LHS in non-negative and the RHS non-positive, which can only be if both of them are zero. Therefore,

$$\lambda(p - q)y = 0 \Rightarrow y = 0. \tag{2.62}$$

From the budget constraint, $x = w/p$. Now we can find $\mu_1 = 0$, $\lambda = 1/p$, $\mu_2 = q/p - 1 > 0$. Multiplying (2.60) by x

$$-\mu_2 x = \lambda(p - q)x. \tag{2.63}$$

If $p > q$, then the LHS in non-positive and the RHS non-negative, which can only be if both of them are zero. Therefore,

$$\lambda(p - q)x = 0 \Rightarrow x = 0. \tag{2.64}$$

From the budget constraint, $y = w/q$. Now we can find $\mu_2 = 0$, $\lambda = 1/q$, $\mu_1 = p/q - 1 > 0$. Finally, if $p = q$ then $\mu_1 = \mu_2 = 0$ (they cannot be both positive, since it will imply that $x = y = 0$, which contradicts the fact that the budget constraint binds). In that case, $\lambda = 1/p$ and x and y are any non-negative numbers such that $px + qy = w$. Therefore, we again obtain the same solution as in the first approach.

Contrary to the case we just considered were goods were perfect substitutes, our next example considers the case, when the individual wishes to consume goods in a fixed proportion.

Example 19. Let an individual's utility function be given by

$$u(x, y) = \min(x, y). \tag{2.65}$$

These preferences are known as *Leontieff preferences and goods are known as perfect complements.* For example, if x is sugar and y is coffee, and the consumer drinks every cup of coffee with a piece of sugar, does not enjoy coffee without sugar and has no other use of sugar, her utility will be determined by the minimum of the number of cups of coffee and pieces of sugar she can afford. Let $p > 0$ and $q > 0$ be the prices of goods x and y and $w > 0$ the individual's wealth.

To find the individual's demand for x and y solve:

$$\max \min(x, y), \tag{2.66}$$

$$\text{s.t. } px + qy \leq w, \ x \geq 0, \ y \geq 0. \tag{2.67}$$

Since the utility function is not differentiable, one cannot use the method of Lagrange multipliers to solve the problem. To solve it, first note that the non-negativity constraints do not bind (the argument is the same as in the Cobb–Douglas case). The budget constraint, on the other hand binds, because if the individual is left with some money spending it, for example, equally on both goods will increase her utility. At optimum $x = y$. Indeed, if $x > y$, then $u(x, y) = y$. By selling a little bit of x, so it still remains greater then y and using it to buy more of good y the individual will move to a new bundle (x', y') with both x' and y' greater then y. Therefore, $u(x', y') > y = u(x, y)$. Similarly, we can rule out the case, $y > x$. Therefore,

$$x = y = \frac{w}{p + q}. \tag{2.68}$$

If $p' \cdot x(p, w) \leq w'$, and $x(p, w) \neq x(p', w')$ then $p \cdot x(p', w') > w$.

2.5   Advanced topics in consumer theory: indirect utility and hicksian demand*

In this section, I am going to discuss two useful identities in the consumer theory: the Roy's identity and the Slutsky equation.

2.5.1   *The Roy's identity*

I start with deriving the famous identity that links the Marshallian demand to the indirect utility function. Assume, consumer's preferences are given by a continuously differentiable utility function $u(x)$. Define the indirect utility function:

$$v(w, p) = \max u(x), \tag{2.69}$$
$$\text{s.t. } x \geq 0, \ p \cdot x \leq w. \tag{2.70}$$

Let $x(p, w)$ be the solution to this problem. It is called Marshallian demand.

$$x(p, w) = -\frac{\partial v / \partial p}{\partial v / \partial w}. \tag{2.71}$$

Note that, $\partial v / \partial w = \lambda$ that is the economic meaning of Lagrange multiplier in this problem is *marginal utility of income*. In general, economic meaning of Lagrange multiplier is the marginal value of relaxing the constraint. Indirect utility is defined by:

$$v(p, w) = \max u(x), \tag{2.72}$$
$$\text{s.t. } p \cdot x \leq w_i, \ x \geq 0. \tag{2.73}$$

It is linked to the Marshallian demand through the *Roy's identity*

$$x_i(p, w_i) = -\frac{\partial v/\partial p_i}{\partial v/\partial w}.$$

The identity can be used to recover indirect utility from demand by solving a system of partial differential equations or proving that the demand does not come from utility maximization if the system turns out to be incompatible. If one is able to invert the demand function to write prices and wealth in terms of bundle demanded, one can use Roy's identity to recover utility from the demand.

2.5.2 *The dual problem*

If a price of a good increases, it affects the demand for the good through two channels. First, the relative prices of goods change, which creates an incentive to substitute away from the good. This effect is known as the *substitution effect*. Second, the real income changes, which has an ambiguous effect on the demand depending on whether the good is normal or inferior. This effect is known as the *income effect.*

To separate the income and the substitution effect, it is useful to consider the following expenditure minimization problem, also known as the *dual* problem

$$\min(p \cdot x), \tag{2.74}$$

$$\text{s.t. } u(x) \geq \overline{u}. \tag{2.75}$$

The solution to this problem is usually denoted by $h(p, \overline{u})$ and is known as the Hicksian (*compensated*) demand. The value function of this problem is known as the *expenditure* function, $e(p, \overline{u})$. By the envelope theorem for constraint optimization

$$h_i(p, \overline{u}) = \frac{\partial e(p, \overline{u})}{\partial p_i}. \tag{2.76}$$

Expenditure function is concave as the lower envelope of linear functions, therefore the Hicksian demand is downward slopping. Note that this implies that the Jacobian matrix

$$J_{ij} = \frac{\partial h_i}{\partial p_j}, \tag{2.77}$$

must be symmetric and negatively semidefinite.

The connection between Marshallian and Hicksian demands is,

$$\begin{cases} x(p, e(p, \overline{u})) = h(p, \overline{u}), \\ x(p, w) = h(p, v(p, w)). \end{cases} \tag{2.78}$$

Let us study identity (2.78) for a concrete numerical example, using Excel. Open Chapter_2.xlsx (Available at: http://www.worldscientific.com/worldscibooks/10.1142/10138) sheet Hicksian Demand. The utility function is the same as on the sheet Marshallian Demand, but now we take utility level as given and are trying to minimize expenditure. In that file, cells B5 and C5 are designated as variable cells, and coefficients α and β are in cells B6 and C6, respectively. Cell D6, the constraint cell, has the formula (2.42) programmed into it, prices are in the cells B9 and C9 and the expenditure is programmed into cell D9. When you run the Solver, do not forget to click *Set Objective to Min*. Now fix prices and coefficients α and β at the same values as on the sheet Marshallian Demand and set Target Utility equal to the maximized value you obtained while finding the Marshallian demand, i.e., let $p = q = 1$, $\alpha = 0.5$, $\beta = 0.3$, $\overline{u} = 1.381022$. If you now run the Solver, you will obtain $x = 4.08$, $y = 3.92$, in accordance with (2.78). Note also that the minimal expenditure is equal to 8, the budget you were allocated when you were asked to find the Marshallian demand.

To study the decomposition of the total price effect, suppose price vector changed from p to p', while wealth stated on the same level. To calculate the substitution effect, define $\overline{u} = u(x(p, w))$ and calculate the Hicksian demand $h(p', \overline{u})$. Then the substitution effect is given by

$$h(p', \overline{u}) - x(p, w).$$

The full effect of price change is,

$$x(p', w) - x(p, w) = (h(p', \overline{u}) - x(p, w)) + (x(p', w) - h(p', w)). \tag{2.79}$$

The first term in (2.79) represents the substitution effect (SE), therefore the second stands for income effect (IE). If only the price of good i changes and the price change is infinitesimally small, the vector of SEs is given by:

$$\mathrm{SE} = \frac{\partial h}{\partial p_i}.$$

Decomposition of the effect of the infinitesimal price change into the income and the substitution effects is achieved by Slutsky equation

$$\frac{\partial x_i}{\partial p_j} = \frac{\partial h_i}{\partial p_j} - x_j \frac{\partial x_i}{\partial w}. \tag{2.80}$$

The first term on the RHS represents the SE and is always non-positive if $i = j$ (SE for the own price change), the second term represents the income effect. If a good is normal, the income and the substitution effect work in the same direction and the demand for the good is downward slopping. Therefore, for a good to be Giffen, it should be inferior.

Equation (2.80) allows one to reconstruct Jacobian matrix (2.77) from the observable demand data. Testing whether this matrix is symmetric and negatively semidefinite, one can test the hypothesis of utility maximization.

2.6 Problems

(1) Assume utility function has a form

$$u(x, y) = (x^\rho + y^\rho)^{1/\rho}. \tag{2.81}$$

(a) Define elasticity of substitution between goods x and y as

$$\varepsilon = -\frac{d\ln(x/y)}{d\ln(p/q)}, \tag{2.82}$$

where p is the price of good x and q in the price of good y. Show that for this utility function

$$\varepsilon = \frac{1}{1-\rho}. \tag{2.83}$$

Note that the elasticity is constant, therefore function (2.81) is known as *constant elasticity of substitution* (*CES*) function.

(b) Find Marshallian demand.

(c) What is the Marshallian demand in the following special cases: $\rho = 1$, $\rho \to +0$, $\rho \to +\infty$?

(2)* Consider the same utility as in Problem 1 and repeat (b) and (c) for Hicksian demand.

(3) Consider utility

$$u(x, y) = \gamma(x^\rho + y^\rho)^{1/\rho} + (1 - \gamma)x^{1/3}y^{2/3}. \tag{2.84}$$

Set up an Excel spreadsheet and find the demand for $\rho = 0.5$, $p = 1$, $q = 2$, $w = 10$ and $\gamma \in \{0, 0.2, 0.4, 0.6, 0.8, 1\}$. In cases $\gamma \in \{0, 1\}$, derive the general formula for the demand and compare the value obtained from the formula with one you found using Excel.

(4) Assume the consumer's utility has a form

$$u(x, y) = x + \ln y.$$

(a) Find the Marshallian demand, the indirect utility, and verify the Roy's identity.

(b) Find the Hicksian demand, the expenditure function, and verify the Slutsky equation.

Chapter 3

The Producer Theory

In this chapter, we discuss the producer theory. While the consumer theory discussed in the previous chapter provided us with the mechanism of formation of the demand, the producer theory aims at explaining the origins of supply. The basic production unit in an economy is called a *firm*. For the purposes of this chapter, the internal structure of the firm is considered to be a black box and the firm is identified with its technology captured by the production function. Firms are simply assumed to choose production plans to maximize profits, taking both input and output prices as given. These profit maximizing plans give rise to the supply function, which maps the output prices into production decisions.

There are three issues that are side-stepped in the model of profit maximization. The first one, separation of ownership and control, will be discussed later in this book, once we reach the topic of economics of information. Another issue is the difference in the risk attitudes among shareholders. This issue is relevant for the corporate firms. However, it does not arise if the capital markets are perfect. Discussion of this issue is more appropriate for a corporate finance class, and the issue will not be discussed here. The final issue is that of the boundaries of a firm. This issue is still a subject of active research. Detailed study of this research is the subject of more advanced classes such as contract theory. Here, I will only offer some brief comments on the issue.

Many transactions between firms take time to complete. Parties cannot imagine all possible contingencies in advance, i.e., they are bounded rational. As a result, the contracts are incomplete. It is still an open research question how exactly does bounded rationality lead to the contractual incompleteness, though some promising models emerged during the previous two decades.[1] Contractual incompleteness leads to the hold-up problem, since parties make a relation specific investment (e.g., seat assembly manufacturer can locate closely to a car manufacturer, a power plant can locate closely to a coal mine). The ways to overcome the hold-up problem are the unified governance (e.g., Ford Motors, General Motors). The major drawback of this approach is that high powered market incentives are replaced by lower powered incentives within an organization. The other approach is that of using relational contracts, where parties have a long-term relation and long time horizon and rely on reputation to facilitate economic transactions. Sometimes it may also be beneficial to rely on social norms.

3.1 A neoclassical firm

A neoclassical firm is an organization that produces goods or services. One can distinguish the following organizational forms. A sole proprietorship is a firm owned by a single person. A partnership is a firm owned by more than one person; partners decide the division of income and are liable for losses. A corporation, in contrast to a partnership, is characterized by limited liability on the part of numerous small owners. Any firm, even the sole proprietorship, usually consists of many individuals, whose objectives are not necessarily the same. This problem, however, becomes more severe as we move from sole proprietorship to corporation, since ownership becomes more and more separated from the control. The basic neoclassical model abstracts of these issues endows the firm with a well-defined objective. We will return to these issue later in the course.

From the neoclassical point of view, each firm is simply a technology that transforms factors of production (e.g., capital, labor, raw materials) into final goods. For simplicity of exposition, we assume that each firm produces a single output good. The production technology is captured by the production function

$$y = F(x), \tag{3.1}$$

where y is the output and $x = (x_1, \ldots, x_n)$ is the vector of inputs and $F(x)$ is weakly increasing in all inputs. The firm is always a price taker

---

[1]Another reason advanced for the contractual incompleteness is so-called *ambiguity aversion* that stipulates that economic agents prefer uncertain situation with known odds to similar situations with odds unknown.

on the input market, i.e., it takes the prices of the factors of production $w = (w_1, \ldots, w_n)$ as given. A competitive firm is also a price taker on the output market. However, having in mind applications to the theory of monopoly and oligopoly, let us formulate the firms problem in the following way: the firm maximizes profits, π, given by:

$$\pi = p(y)F(x) - w \cdot x,$$
$$\text{s.t. } y = F(x), \; x_i \geq 0. \tag{3.2}$$

In this formulation, we allow for the price of the firm's output to depend on the latter. If we further assume that $p(y) = p$, i.e., the firm is price taker on the output market, then we can define the solution to the firm's problem, $x(p, w)$. It is known as the factor demand and the corresponding value of the output $y = F(x(p, w))$ is known as the supply.

The Lagrangian for the profit maximizing problem for a competitive firm is:

$$L = pf(x) - w \cdot x + \mu \cdot x. \tag{3.3}$$

Here vector μ is the vector of Lagrange multipliers on the non-negativity constraints. The first-order conditions are

$$p\frac{\partial f}{\partial x_i} = w_i - \mu_i,$$
$$\mu_i \geq 0, \; \mu_i x_i = 0. \tag{3.4}$$

If all factors of production are used ($x_i > 0$ for all i)

$$\frac{w_i}{w_j} = \frac{\partial f/\partial x_i}{\partial f/\partial x_j}. \tag{3.5}$$

The RHS of this equation is called the marginal rate of technological substitution (MRTS).

To understand the geometric meaning of the MRTS, let us first define an isoquant as the locus of points

$$f(x) = \text{const.} \tag{3.6}$$

Following the same logic as we did in the previous chapter for the indifference curves, we come to the conclusion that MRTS is the slope of the isoquant. Similarly, from the economic point of view, MRTS measures how much more of input x_1 you need to get compensated for the loss of a unit of good x_2 in order to be able to produce the same output.

Note that the firm's problem resembles the consumer problem with one difference: there is *no* budget constraint. Therefore, when the prices of the inputs and the output change, the only kind of effect is the substitution effect. For example, if the wage increases, firms will substitute away from labor to capital.

Therefore,

$$\frac{\partial x_i}{\partial w_i} < 0, \quad \frac{\partial y}{\partial p} > 0. \tag{3.7}$$

The second of these inequalities is known as the law of supply. The law of supply always holds, there is no analog of Giffen goods.

By the envelope theorem for constraint maximization,

$$\frac{\partial \pi}{\partial w_i} = -x_i(w).$$

For a competitive firm:

$$\frac{\partial \pi}{\partial p} = y.$$

That is, supply of the good is the derivative of profits. By the convexity of profits, the supply curve is always upward slopping. These equations together are known as the *Hotelling's lemma*. They are the counterparts of Roy's identity in the consumer theory.

3.1.1   *Cobb–Douglas production function*

Assume a competitive firm produces an output using two inputs: x_1 — capital and x_2 — labor. Let the production function have the Cobb–Douglas form

$$f(x) = x_1^\alpha x_2^\beta, \tag{3.8}$$

where

$$\alpha > 0, \quad \beta > 0. \tag{3.9}$$

Let us consider three different scenarios.

Decreasing Returns to Scale Technology

Let us assume that parameters of the production function satisfy:

$$\alpha + \beta < 1. \tag{3.10}$$

Note that in this case

$$f(\lambda x_1, \lambda x_2) = \lambda^{\alpha+\beta} f(x_1, x_2) < f(x_1, x_2), \qquad (3.11)$$

provided $\lambda < 1$. Production functions that satisfy (3.11) are said to exhibit *decreasing returns to scale*. Then profits are,

$$\pi(p, w) = \max_{x_1, x_2}(px_1^\alpha x_2^\beta - w_1 x_1 - w_2 x_2). \qquad (3.12)$$

The first-order conditions for the profit maximization take the form:

$$\begin{cases} \alpha p x_1^{\alpha-1} x_2^\beta = w_1, \\ \beta p x_1^\alpha x_2^{\beta-1} = w_2. \end{cases}$$

Dividing one by the other[2]

$$\frac{\alpha x_2}{\beta x_1} = \frac{w_1}{w_2}. \qquad (3.13)$$

Solving for x_2 and substituting into the first equation in the system:

$$\alpha p \left(\frac{\beta w_1}{\alpha w_2}\right)^\beta x_1^{\alpha+\beta-1} = w_1. \qquad (3.14)$$

Finally

$$\begin{cases} x_1 = \alpha^{\frac{1-\beta}{1-\alpha-\beta}} \beta^{\frac{\beta}{1-\alpha-\beta}} \left(\frac{p}{w_1^{1-\beta} w_2^\beta}\right)^{\frac{1}{1-\alpha-\beta}}, \\ x_2 = \beta^{\frac{1-\alpha}{1-\alpha-\beta}} \alpha^{\frac{\alpha}{1-\alpha-\beta}} \left(\frac{p}{w_1^\alpha w_2^{1-\alpha}}\right)^{\frac{1}{1-\alpha-\beta}}, \qquad (3.15) \\ y = \alpha^{\frac{\alpha}{1-\alpha-\beta}} \beta^{\frac{\beta}{1-\alpha-\beta}} \left(\frac{p^{\alpha+\beta}}{w_1^\alpha w_2^\beta}\right)^{\frac{1}{1-\alpha-\beta}}. \end{cases}$$

3.1.2 *Constant returns to scale*

Let us assume that parameters of the production function satisfy:

$$\alpha + \beta = 1. \qquad (3.16)$$

---

[2]It is obvious that $x_i = 0$ cannot be the profit maximizing choice, since the output will be zero and the profits are positive for sufficiently small positive value of both factors due to the condition (3.10).

Note that in this case

$$f(\lambda x_1, \lambda x_2) = \lambda f(x_1, x_2). \tag{3.17}$$

Production functions that satisfy (3.17) are said to exhibit constant returns to scale. The firm solves

$$\max_{x_1, x_2}(px_1^\alpha x_2^{1-\alpha} - w_1 x_1 - w_2 x_2).$$

The first-order conditions for the profit maximization, ignoring the non-negativity constraints, take the form:

$$\begin{cases} \alpha p \left(\frac{x_2}{x_1}\right)^{1-\alpha} = w_1, \\ (1-\alpha)p \left(\frac{x_1}{x_2}\right)^{\alpha} = w_2. \end{cases}$$

Note that both conditions give us some restriction on the same ratio x_1/x_2. Therefore, in general, we cannot satisfy them simultaneously. A profit maximizing plan that *uses both inputs* generically does not exist. To find the solution to the firm's problem, let us rewrite the profits in a form

$$\pi = x_1(pz^{1-\alpha} - w_1 - w_2 z), \tag{3.18}$$

where

$$z = \frac{x_2}{x_1}.$$

Let us fix x_1 and solve for optimal z. For example, given the amount of capital, how much labor to hire?

The first-order condition for this problem is

$$(1-\alpha)pz^{-\alpha} = w_2. \tag{3.19}$$

Solving for z and substituting into profit function,

$$\pi = \frac{x_1 w_1}{\alpha}\left(1 - \alpha - \frac{w_2 w_1^{\frac{1}{1-\alpha}}}{\alpha^{1-\alpha}p^{1-\alpha}}\right) = Ax_1,$$

where

$$A = \frac{w_1}{\alpha}\left(1 - \alpha - \frac{w_2 w_1^{\frac{1}{1-\alpha}}}{\alpha^{1-\alpha}p^{1-\alpha}}\right). \tag{3.20}$$

Three cases are possible.

Case 1. Let us assume that,

$$(1-\alpha)^{1-\alpha}\alpha^{\alpha}p > w_1^{\alpha}w_2^{1-\alpha}. \tag{3.21}$$

In this case $A > 0$ and optimal $x_1 = \infty$. The firm uses all the resources it can put its hands on. Output is as big as possible (ideally, infinite), i.e., $y = \infty$.

Case 2. Let us assume that,

$$(1-\alpha)^{1-\alpha}\alpha^{\alpha}p = w_1^{\alpha}w_2^{1-\alpha}. \tag{3.22}$$

In this case $A = 0$ and profits are identically zero. The firm does not care how much of inputs to use as long as they are in the proportion given by the (3.19). Therefore, factor demand is a correspondence, rather than a function an is given by:

$$\begin{aligned} x_1 &\in [0,\infty), \\ x_2 &\in [0,\infty), \\ x_2/x_1 &= z. \end{aligned} \tag{3.23}$$

Supply is also a correspondence

$$y \in [0,\infty). \tag{3.24}$$

Case 3. Let us assume that,

$$(1-\alpha)^{1-\alpha}\alpha^{\alpha}p < w_1^{\alpha}w_2^{1-\alpha}. \tag{3.25}$$

In this case $A < 0$, so firm loses money if it produces anything. Therefore,

$$x_1 = x_2 = y = 0. \tag{3.26}$$

The situation of this example is typical for constant returns to scale functions.

3.2 Production possibilities frontier of an economy

Consider an economy in which two goods can be produced, computers, Y_1, and apples, Y_2, using a single input, labor, L. Production technologies are

$$\begin{aligned} Y_1 &= F_1(L_1), \\ Y_2 &= F_2(L_2), \end{aligned} \tag{3.27}$$

where L_i is the amount of labor devoted to the production of Y_i. The total amount of labor available to the economy is L. Then each unit of labor put into the production of computers means that there is less labor available to produce apples.

The total amount of apples that the economy can produce if it utilizes all its labor is a decreasing function of the total amount of computers it produce.

$$Y_2 = G(Y_1). \tag{3.28}$$

The graph of this function is called the *production possibilities frontier* (*PPF*) of the economy. A real economy will produce at a point below the PPF due to different inefficiencies. In factors allocations, the closeness of the actual production point to the PPF is a measure of the productive efficiency of the economy.

3.2.1 *Marginal rate of technological transformation*

The absolute value of slope of the PPF is known as marginal rate of technological transformation (MRTT).

$$\text{MRTT} = -\frac{dY_2}{dY_1} = \frac{dY_2/dL_1}{dY_1/dL_2} = \frac{F_1'(L_1)}{F_2'(L_2)} = \frac{MP_L^1}{MP_L^1}.$$

(sign — appears after the first equality sign because the slope is negative, it disappears after the second, since $L_1 + L_2 = L$ implies $dL_1 = -dL_2$), i.e., MRTT is the ratio of marginal products of labor.

Example 1. Let

$$Y_1 = \sqrt{L_1}, \tag{3.29}$$
$$Y_2 = \sqrt{L_2}, \tag{3.30}$$
$$L_1 + L_2 = L = 1. \tag{3.31}$$

Then,

$$L_1 - Y_1^2, \tag{3.32}$$
$$L_2 = Y_2^2, \tag{3.33}$$

and PPF has the form

$$Y_1^2 + Y_2^2 = 1. \tag{3.34}$$

Since economic meaning of Y_i means that they cannot be negative, geometrically it is the quarter of the unit circle located in the positive quadrant.

3.3 Hotelling Lemma*

In consumer theory, we had a relationship between the indirect utility and Marshallian demand. Similarly, in the producer theory it is possible to establish a relationship between the profit function and the supply. Recall that the firm's profits are defined as

$$\pi(p, w) = \max(py - w \cdot x)$$
$$\text{s.t. } y = f(x). \tag{3.35}$$

It follows immediately from the definition that the profit is convex in both input and output prices. Moreover, the envelope theorem for the constraint optimization implies:

$$y(p, w) = \frac{\partial \pi}{\partial p}. \tag{3.36}$$

This relationship is known as the Hotelling Lemma. Convexity of the profit function then implies that the supply is upward slopping in the output price. Similarly,

$$x_i(p, w) = \frac{\partial \pi}{\partial w_i}, \tag{3.37}$$

therefore unconditional factor demand is downward slopping in the respective input price.

3.4 Conditional cost

Often it is important to separate two different aspects of production plan: how much of a good to produce and what combination of inputs to use given the production plan. The optimal amount of production depends on the structure of the output market: a firm will choose to produce different quantity of good if it is a monopoly than if it is a competitive firm, a generally yet a different quantity if it is a competitor in an oligopolistic market. On the other end, if a firm decides to produce a given quantity, the optimal utilization of inputs does not depend on the structure of the output market. To achieve this end, we will introduce the concept of *conditional cost*.

Conditional (variable) cost is defined by:

$$C(w, y) = \min(w \cdot x)$$
$$\text{s.t. } y = f(x).$$

Note that conditional cost is determined by technology (production function) only.[3]

The envelope theorem for constraint optimization leads to the following result, known as *the Shepard's Lemma*:

$$x_i(w, y) = \frac{\partial C(w, y)}{\partial w_i}, \tag{3.38}$$

or in terms of cost shares:

$$s_i \equiv \frac{w_i x_i}{C} = \frac{\partial \ln C(w, y)}{\partial \ln w_i}.$$

Total cost of production

$$\text{TC}(w, y) = \begin{cases} 0, & \text{if } y = 0, \\ F + C(w, y), & \text{if } y > 0. \end{cases}$$

That is: if the firm stays out of business it incurs no costs, if it decides to be in business in pays a fixed set-up cost F, and total variable conditional cost: $C(w, y)$. Below I assume w to be fixed and omit it as an argument, so I write $C(y)$ instead of $C(w, y)$, and $\text{TC}(y)$ instead of $\text{TC}(w, y)$.

$$\text{MC}(y) = C'(y),$$
$$\text{AC}(y) = \frac{\text{TC}(y)}{y}, \quad y > 0.$$

Here, $\text{MC}(y)$ is the marginal cost of production and $\text{AC}(y)$ is the average cost.

---

[3]Moreover, a quasiconcave production function can be uniquely retrieved from the conditional cost.

Assume that $C(y)$ is strictly convex and $C'(0) = 0$. Then a competitive firm produce at a unique level y^* determined by $MC(y^*) = p$, provided $AC(y^*) \leq p$ and stays out of business otherwise.

Let y_m be the minimum of average cost. At this point $AC(y_m) = MC(y_m)$. The supply correspondence is

$$y(p) = \begin{cases} 0, & \text{if } p < AC(y_m), \\ \{0, y_m\}, & \text{if } p = AC(y_m), \\ MC^{-1}(p), & \text{if } p > AC(y_m). \end{cases} \qquad (3.39)$$

3.5 Problems

(1) Assume that an economy can produce two goods: cars and bananas and labor is the only factor of production. Production technology for the cars is given by production function:

$$x = \sqrt{L}, \qquad (3.40)$$

and for bananas by:

$$y = L. \qquad (3.41)$$

There are L^* units of labor in the economy. Find the production possibilities frontier.

(2) A firm produces a good, q, using two factors of production capital and labor and technology, given by production function:

$$q = F(K, L). \qquad (3.42)$$

Assuming wage rate is w and rental rate of capital is r, find conditional cost and conditional factor demands for the following technologies:

(a) Leontieff technology:

$$F(K, L) = \min(K, L). \qquad (3.43)$$

(b)

$$F(K, L) = (aK^\rho + bL^\rho)^{\frac{\gamma}{\rho}}. \qquad (3.44)$$

(c)

$$F(K, L) = K + L. \qquad (3.45)$$

(3) Assume

$$F(K, L) = \eta(aK^\rho + bL^\rho)^{\frac{1}{\rho}} + (1 - \eta) \min(K, L). \qquad (3.46)$$

Let $w = r = 1$ and $p = 2$, where p is the price of output. Develop Excel spreadsheet to find the optimal level of production for $\eta \in \{0, 0.2, 0.4, 0.6, 0.8, 1\}$. For $\eta \in \{0, 1\}$, verify your numerical result by comparing it to an explicit analytical solution you obtained in Problem 2.

Chapter 4

General Equilibrium

In this chapter, we bring together the consumers and the producers and get them to interact through the markets. We start with a simple model of production and assume for simplicity that there is just one agent in the economy who acts as both a consumer and a competitive firm. This is the so-called Robinson Crusoe economy. The point of this exercise is to highlight role of prices in deciding how much to produce. Next, we move to the equilibria in pure exchange economy without production. The point of this exercise is to highlight role of prices in deciding how to distribute produced resources between the consumers.

4.1 The Robinson Crusoe's economy

Robinson Crusoe lives on a desert island. He has a unit of time per day, which he can divide between leisure (good x_1) and collecting coconuts (good x_2). Since he is bored, he plays the following game with himself: first he sets a price for a coconut and a wage for an hour spent collecting. As a consumer, he makes a decision how much time to spend collecting coconuts and how many coconuts to eat given the wage and the price of coconuts, as a firm he decides how much coconuts to produce given their price and the wage. The question is: Is there a price and a wage such as all decisions made by Robinson Crusoe are compatible?

Example 1. Assume Robinson's utility is,

$$u(x_1, x_2) = x_1 x_2,$$

and production function for coconuts is,

$$y_2 = \sqrt{L_2},$$

where L_2 is the time spent collecting coconuts. We will also assume that Robinson the consumer owns the firm, so his income consists of the wage income and profits. Normalizing the total endowment of time to be one, Robinson as a consumer will solve

$$\max x_1 x_2$$
$$\text{s.t. } px_2 \leq wL_2 + \pi(p, w)$$
$$L_2 + x_1 = 1, L_2 \geq 0, x_2 \geq 0.$$

The solution to this problem is,

$$x_1 = \frac{w + \pi(p, w)}{2w}, \quad x_2 = \frac{w + \pi(p, w)}{2p}.$$

Robinson acting as the firm solves:

$$\max(p\sqrt{L_2} - wL_2).$$

The solution is,

$$L_2 = \frac{p^2}{4w^2}, \quad y = \frac{p}{2w}, \quad \pi(p, w) = \frac{p^2}{4w}.$$

In equilibrium, the amount of coconuts produced should be equal to the amount consumed (supply equals demand):

$$\frac{w + \pi(p, w)}{2p} = \frac{p}{2w}.$$

Plugging $\pi(p, w) = \frac{p^2}{4w}$ and solving, one obtains,

$$\frac{w}{p} = \frac{\sqrt{3}}{2} \quad x_1 = \frac{2}{3}, \quad L_2 = \frac{1}{3}, \quad y = x_2 = \frac{1}{\sqrt{3}}.$$

4.2 The pure exchange economy

Assume there are L goods and I consumers. Consumer i has an endowment $\omega_i = (\omega_{i1}, \ldots, \omega_{iL})$, which she sells at the market at price p and obtains wealth $w_i = p \cdot \omega_i$. We will assume that endowments are strictly positive, so that each consumer always has positive wealth. Then the consumer buys goods for her consumption at the same price (she may buy back some of the goods she sold). The Marshallian demand of a consumer with wealth w_i is $x_i(p, w_i)$. Define the excess demand vector by:

$$z(p) = \sum_{i=1}^{I}(x_i(p, p \cdot \omega_i) - \omega_i).$$

Definition 2. A vector $p \in R^L$ is said to clear the market if,

$$z(p) = 0.$$

Excess demand is HD(0) and if preferences are strictly monotone, the excess demand satisfies Walras law.

$$p \cdot z(p) = 0 \text{ for any } p.$$

If p^* clears the market, then price-allocation pair $(p^*, x_i(p^*, p^* \cdot \omega_i))$ is called Walrasian equilibrium (WE) and the allocation $x_i(p^*, p^* \cdot \omega_i)$ is called the WE allocation. Walras law implies that it is sufficient to solve market clearing equations for $L - 1$ markets. If $L = 2$, it is sufficient to consider just one market. Note that as the relative price of a good goes to zero, the demand for it goes to infinity, since preferences are assumed to be strictly monotone. Therefore, as p_1/p_2 goes to zero, z_1 becomes a big positive number, *vice versa* as p_1/p_2 goes to infinity (so that p_2/p_1 goes to zero) z_2 goes to infinity, and hence by Walras law z_1 is negative. Therefore, if z is continuous, equilibrium exists. Existence can be proved under rather general conditions[1] for an economy containing arbitrary finite number of goods and consumers. Let us consider the following example.

Example 3. Assume there are two consumers: Ann and Bob and two goods, bananas (good x) and apples (good y). Ann's utility function is:

$$u_A(x_A, y_A) = x_A y_A \tag{4.1}$$

and her endowment is:

$$\omega_A = (2, 1). \tag{4.2}$$

Bob's utility function is:

$$u_B(x_B, y_B) = x_B^2 y_B \tag{4.3}$$

---

[1]These conditions are that utility function are quasiconcave and continuous and endowments are strictly positive.

and his endowment is:

$$\omega_B = (1, 1). \tag{4.4}$$

To find equilibrium, assume that equilibrium price vector is

$$p = (p_x, p_y). \tag{4.5}$$

Since demand is HD(0) without loss of generality one can set $p_x = 1$, and write $q = p_y$. Then Ann's wealth[2] at this prices is:

$$w_A = 2 + q. \tag{4.6}$$

In Section 2.4, we have found the demand for the consumer with Cobb–Douglas preferences:

$$u(x, y) = x^\alpha y^{1-\alpha}. \tag{4.7}$$

At first glance, Ann's and Bob's preferences have a more general form

$$u(x, y) = x^\alpha y^\beta. \tag{4.8}$$

However, note that

$$x^\alpha y^\beta = \left(x^{\frac{\alpha}{\alpha+\beta}} * y^{\frac{\beta}{\alpha+\beta}} \right)^{\alpha+\beta}, \tag{4.9}$$

therefore utility (4.8) captures the same preference relation as utility

$$u(x, y) = x^{\frac{\alpha}{\alpha+\beta}} * y^{\frac{\beta}{\alpha+\beta}}. \tag{4.10}$$

(prove the last assertion). Therefore, Ann's demand for banana's and apples is given by:

$$x_A = \frac{2+q}{2}, \quad y_A = \frac{2+q}{2q}. \tag{4.11}$$

Similarly, Bob's wealth at the market prices is:

$$w_B = 1 + q \tag{4.12}$$

and his demand for banana's and apples is given by:

$$x_B = \frac{2(1+q)}{3}, \quad y_B = \frac{1+q}{3q}. \tag{4.13}$$

---

[2]It is obtained by evaluating value of her endowment at market prices.

Total demand for bananas therefore is:

$$x_A + x_B = \frac{2+q}{2} + \frac{2(1+q)}{3} = \frac{7}{6}q + \frac{5}{3}. \qquad (4.14)$$

The total supply of banana's is the sum of Ann's and Bob's endowments, and is equal to 3. Therefore demand equals supply if and only if:

$$\frac{7}{6}q + \frac{5}{3} = 3 \Rightarrow q = \frac{8}{7}. \qquad (4.15)$$

By Walras law, if the market for bananas clears, so does market for apples. Verify by a direct calculation that this is indeed the case.

4.3 Role of prices in ensuring optimality of Walrasian allocation

We considered economies with both production and consumption activities but without exchange and the one with pure exchange and no production. In general, economy will contain both production activities and exchange. In a similar fashion, one can establish existence and in simple cases compute equilibrium prices. Note that prices play three fold role in an economy: they equate marginal rates of substitution of goods between all the consumers. So, once goods are produced, there is no way to start with a Walrasian equilibrium allocation and redistribute goods among to consumers to make everyone better off. On the margin, everyone values the goods in proportion to their prices. The prices also equate marginal costs of production across firms, ensuring that the goods are produced by the economy at the minimal cost. One cannot relocate production from firm A to firm B and reduce the total cost, since on the margin, producing every unit at any firm is equally costly. Finally, by equating marginal rate of substitution between goods to the marginal rate of technological transformation, the price mechanism ensures that correct amount of goods is produced at equilibrium. These three properties are summarized by saying that Walrasian equilibrium allocation is *Pareto optimal* (PO), i.e., it is impossible to change it in such a way as to make some economic agents (consumers or producers) better off, without making any agent worse off. This result is known as the First Welfare Theorem. I will close this chapter by formally defining Pareto optimality and stating the First Welfare Theorem.

Definition 4. An allocation is Pareto optimal if there exists no other feasible allocation that makes some agents better off without making anyone worse off.

Theorem 5 (First Theorem of Welfare Economics). *Assume everyone strictly prefers more to less.*[3] *Then the Walrasian equilibrium allocation is PO.*[4]

The first welfare theorem guarantees that any Walrasian equilibrium is Pareto optimal. One can ask a reverse question: given a Pareto optimal allocation is it possible to support it as a Walrasian equilibrium? The answer to this question is also positive, but the technical conditions are more stringent. On the technical side, one has to assume that in addition to the conditions of the first welfare theorem that both preferences and technologies are convex. More importantly, on the conceptual side, one has to assume that lump-sum transfers are available. If this is the case, then the following result is true.

Theorem 6 (Second Theorem of Welfare Economics). *Assume that preferences are monotone and convex and technologies are convex. Then given any PO allocation there exits set of lump-sum transfers of wealth such that economy where individual endowments are augmented by these transfers possesses a Walrasian equilibrium allocation that coincides with the given allocation.*

The idea of proof is rather simple. The first-order conditions for Pareto optimality ensure that marginal rates of substitution of goods between all the consumers, marginal costs of production across firms, and marginal rate of substitution between goods to the marginal rate of technological transformation are equal to each other. Define price ratios among the goods equal to these common value and normalizing price of one of the goods to one, define the prices. Then evaluate wealth of each individual in the designed allocation at these prices and their wealth at their endowments and affect lump-sum transfers to the individual equal to the difference in wealth between the desired allocation and the endowment. It is straightforward, if

---

[3]Such preferences are known as monotone. In fact, a weaker property, known as local non-satiation, is sufficient.

[4]Conditions for the First Welfare Theorem are not strong enough to guarantee existence of the equilibrium. However, if an equilibrium exists, it is PO.

somewhat technical, to show that the individual will trade to the desired allocation.

Second welfare theorem was used to argue that a government, which has a distributional objective, has to interfere only once. The problem with this argument is an assumption that the government should possess a lot of information about individual endowments or at least have a way to illicit it without affecting the individuals' behaviors. In practice, any intervention is likely to change behavior. For example, income tax is likely to change labor supply, making taxes based solely on earning ability infeasible. Such considerations gave birth to the theory of second best. The theoretical underpinnings of this theory, information economics, is considered in Part IV of this book.

4.4 Using Excel to compute Walrasian equilibrium

In the case of two goods finding Walrasian equilibrium reduces to solving, in general a nonlinear, equation. Such a procedure can be carried out by Excel. To see how, let us consider the following example.

Example 7. Assume there are two goods in the economy, coffee (good x) and chocolates (good y) and two consumers Alice and Mad Hatter. Alice has utility:

$$u_A(x, y) = x^{1/5} + y \tag{4.16}$$

and endowment $(1, 1)$. Mad Hatter has utility

$$u_{\text{MH}}(x, y) = xy \tag{4.17}$$

and endowment $(0, 3)$. Let us normalize price of chocolates to be one and let p is the price of coffee. Using the same argument as in the previous section, we find the Mad Hatter's demand for coffee to be:

$$x_{\text{MH}} = \frac{3}{2p}. \tag{4.18}$$

Alice's demand solves

$$\begin{aligned} \max(x^{1/5} + y) \\ \text{s.t. } px + y = 1 + p, x \geq 0, y \geq 0. \end{aligned} \tag{4.19}$$

This is equivalent to:

$$\max(x^{1/5} + 1 + p - px) \tag{4.20}$$

subject to the non-negativity constraints. Let us ignore the latter for the moment. Then one can find:

$$\frac{1}{3}x^{-4/5} = p \Rightarrow x_A = (3p)^{-5/4}. \tag{4.21}$$

Equating total demand for coffee to the total supply and collecting all non-zero terms on one side, one obtains:

$$\frac{3}{2p} + (3p)^{-5/4} - 1 = 0. \tag{4.22}$$

Note that since the LHS decreases monotonically in p from infinity to zero the equation possesses a unique solution. However, it cannot be found analytically. Therefore, we will set up a spreadsheet to solve it. Open Chapter_4.xlsx (Available at: http://www.worldscientific.com/worldscibooks/10.1142/10138). In that file cell B5 is designated as variable cells, and endowments of coffee and exponent 1/5 (the parameters of the model we might want to play with) are in cells B9, C9, and B6, respectively. The RHS of Eq. (4.22) is programmed into cell D6. When you run the Solver do not forget to click *Set Value to Zero. Finally, program in cell D9 the following expression for y*

$$y = 1 + p - px \tag{4.23}$$

which will read in Excel

$$D9 = 1 + B5 - B5/(3 * B5)\hat{\ }(1.25). \tag{4.24}$$

This is to check that the value of y is positive for Alice, since we dropped the non-negativity constraint. Running Solver you will get $p = 1.72$ and $y = 2$, so non-negativity constraint is satisfied and $p = 1.72$ is the equilibrium price.

In the example above, we had just two goods. Such approximation can be useful if one looks at economy at aggregate level and divides all the goods into industrial and agricultural produce, for example. Often, however, such approximation is not appropriate. If there are more than two goods, then finding equilibrium prices involves solving a system of equations.

Solver does not have the procedure for doing it.[5] However, note that solving system

$$f_i(p) = 0, i = 1, \ldots, K, p \in R^K \tag{4.25}$$

is equivalent to solving the minimization problem:

$$\min_p \sum_{i=1}^n f_i^2(p). \tag{4.26}$$

Indeed, since for all i:

$$f_i^2(p) \geq 0 \tag{4.27}$$

the sum in (4.26) is minimized at a solution of (4.25). As we discussed above, the Solver can be readily used to handle problem (4.26).

---

[5] One can use matrix algebra to solve a system of linear equations in Excel. We will come to that, when we will discuss the models of oligopoly.

4.5 Problems

(1) Consider the economy with two goods, x and y and two consumers: Ann, with utility

$$u_A(x, y) = x + y \tag{4.28}$$

and endowment $(1, 2)$ and Carl, with utility

$$u_C(x, y) = \min(x, y) \tag{4.29}$$

and endowment $(2, 1)$. Find the equilibrium price ratio. Compare it with Ann's MRS between the goods. What can you conclude?

(2) Consider economy with the same goods and endowments as in Problem 1, but now assume that

$$u_A(x, y) = x^{1/3} + y^{1/3}, \tag{4.30}$$
$$u_C(x, y) = x + \ln y. \tag{4.31}$$

Derive the equation for the equilibrium price in this economy, argue that a solution exists, and find it numerically by building an Excel spreadsheet.

(3) Reconsider the example in the section on Robinson Crusoe's economy, assuming now that Robinson's utility is

$$u(x_1, x_2) = x_1^{1/3} x_2^{2/3}$$

and production function for coconuts is

$$y_2 = L_2^{1/4}.$$

(4) Let

$$u_1(x_{11}, x_{21}) = \ln x_{11} + x_{21},$$
$$u_2(x_{12}, x_{22}) = x_{12}^{1/2} + x_{22}$$

and the initial endowments are

$$\omega_{11} = \omega_{22} = 1,$$
$$\omega_{21} = \omega_{12} = 0.$$

Find the Walrasian equilibria of the economy.

Chapter 5

Choice and Uncertainty

Economic actors are often forced to make choices without full knowledge of the consequences. Consider, for example, the decision whether to take an umbrella with you today. The decision would be easy if you knew whether it will rain. But what should your choice be if you are not sure? Your choice would still be easy if you knew the objective probability that it will rain today. But what if even the probability is not known? The most popular theory in economics, known as subjective expected utility theory, argues that there is no difference between the two situations. Therefore, we will consider in this chapter choice under uncertainty assuming the odds are known. Bibliographic notes in the end of this part will direct you to the references that challenge this assumption.

5.1 Expected utility

Recall that a lottery is a set of outcomes with corresponding probabilities, $L = (x_1, p_1; \ldots; x_n, p_n)$. We want to derive a criterion that allows the individuals to choose among lotteries. Assume the individual has preferences over lotteries that satisfy the following requirements:

(1) (Completeness) For any two lotteries, L_1 and L_2, either $L_1 \succeq L_2$ (reads: L_1 is at least as good as L_2 or L_1 is weakly preferred to L_2) or $L_2 \succeq L_1$.

This axiom says that given any two lotteries, the individual is always able to choose one. Of course, she might be indifferent, in which case she will be willing to take any. But asked, which is better, she never answers: "I do not know."

(2) (Transitivity) For any three lotteries L_1, L_2, and L_3, if $L_1 \succeq L_2$ and $L_2 \succeq L_3$ then $L_1 \succeq L_3$.

This is a very natural consistency requirement. It states that if lottery L_1 is weakly preferred to L_2 and L_2 is weakly preferred to L_3 then L_1 is weakly preferred to L_3.

(3) (Independence) Let $L_1 \succeq L_2$ and $\alpha \in [0,1]$. Then for any lottery $L_3 : \alpha$ $L_1 + (1-\alpha)L_3 \succeq \alpha L_2 + (1-\alpha)L_3$.

To understand the independence axiom suppose you have two lotteries L_1 and L_2 and you weakly prefer L_1 to L_2. Now suppose you are given two choices C_1 and C_2, which are described as follows:

Choice C_1: Flip an unfair coin with probability of H equal to α and probability of T equal to $1-\alpha$. If it comes H up, you will face lottery L_1, if it comes up T, you will face lottery L_3.

Choice C_2: Flip the same coin as in C_1. If it comes H up, you will face lottery L_2, if it comes up T, you will face lottery L_3.

Would you choose C_1 or C_2? Note that if the outcome of the coin flip is T it does not matter which choice had you done, since you face the same lottery L_3 anyway. It only matters if the outcome is H, in which case C_1 will result in you facing L_1 and C_2 in you facing L_2. Since you weakly prefer L_1 to L_2, you should also weakly prefer C_1 over C_2.

Completeness, transitivity, and independence are intuitively appealing requirements. We will call preferences satisfying them CTI preferences. Let $L_1 = (x_1, p_1; \ldots; x_n, p_n)$ and $L_2 = (x_1, q_1; \ldots; x_n, q_n)$. (The assumption that both lotteries have the same set of outcomes is without loss of generality. Indeed, let for example, L_1 be $(0, 1/2; 1, 1/2)$ and $L_2 = (2, 1/3; 3, 2/3)$. Those lotteries have different sets of outcomes. Consider, however, $L_1' = (0, 1/2; 1, 1/2; 2, 0; 3, 0)$ and $L_2' = (0, 0; 1, 0; 2, 1/3; 3, 2/3)$. Then L_1' and L_2' have the same set of outcomes, but L_1' is essentially the same lottery as L_1, since it differs from it only by probability zero outcomes. Similar, L_2' is the same lottery as L_2. Therefore, one can always assume that the set of outcomes is the same). It turns out that if the individuals preferences over lotteries satisfy CTI, then there exists a function $u(\cdot)$ such that,

$$(L_1 \succeq L_2) \Leftrightarrow \sum_{i=1}^{n} p_i u(x_i) \geq \sum_{i=1}^{n} q_i u(x_i). \tag{5.1}$$

Note that in formula (1) we compare *expected values* of some function of payoffs, that is why (1) is called *the expected utility*. Function $u(\cdot)$ is called

Bernoulli utility function. Function $U(\cdot)$ defined by,

$$U(L) = \sum_{i=1}^{n} p_i u(x_i) \tag{5.2}$$

is called von Neumann–Morgenstern utility function.

Note: Bernoulli utility is defined over the monetary payoffs, while von Neumann–Morgenstern utility over the lotteries.

Definition 1. A certainty equivalent of lottery L is defined by:

$$u(\text{CE}) = U(L). \tag{5.3}$$

For example, consider a lottery $(0, 1/2; 1, 1/2)$ and assume an individual has utility function,

$$u(x) = \sqrt{x}. \tag{5.4}$$

Then the certainty equivalent can be found as,

$$\sqrt{\text{CE}} = \frac{1}{2}\sqrt{0} + \frac{1}{2}\sqrt{1} \Rightarrow \text{CE} = \frac{1}{4}. \tag{5.5}$$

5.2 Shape of the Bernoulli utility and risk-aversion

The fact that we transform payoffs using $u(\cdot)$ before calculating the expected value allows us to incorporate preferences for risk into our theory. To see how, assume that the Bernoulli utility function is concave and consider a binary lottery $L_1 = (\alpha, x_1; 1 - \alpha, x_2)$ with the expected value $x = \alpha x_1 + (1 - \alpha) x_2$. Let $L_2 = (x, 1)$ be the lottery that gives x with certainty. Now,

$$U(L_2) = u(x) = u(\alpha x_1 + (1 - \alpha) x_2).$$

By concavity of the Bernoulli utility function,

$$u(\alpha x_1 + (1 - \alpha) x_2) \geq \alpha u(x_1) + (1 - \alpha) u(x_2) = U(L_1).$$

Therefore,

$$U(L_2) \geq U(L_1).$$

Therefore, an individual with concave Bernoulli utility prefers the expected value of the lottery for sure to the lottery itself (the proof can be generalized for more general lotteries). Recall that an individual that prefers the expected value of the lottery for sure to the lottery itself is called risk-averse. Therefore, concavity of the Bernoulli utility is equivalent to the risk-averse behavior. Similarly, convexity of the Bernoulli utility is equivalent to the risk-loving behavior, and linearity of the Bernoulli utility is equivalent to the risk-neutral behavior.

5.3 An example: buying insurance

Suppose a risk averse consumer has wealth $w > 0$. With probability $q > 0$ she may suffer an accident, in which case her wealth will be reduced to $w - D$, for some $D \in (0, w)$. She has an option to buy insurance. If she pays insurance premium x the insurance company will repay her rx in the case of accident for some $r > 1$. Let us find the optimal amount of insurance to buy.

If the consumer purchases amount x of insurance, she will have wealth $w - x$ if no accident happens (probability of this is $1 - q$) and wealth $w - x + rx - D$ if the accident happens (probability of this is q). Therefore, her expected utility is,

$$U(x) = (1 - q)u(w - x) + qu(w - x + rx - D).$$

Note that $U(\cdot)$ is concave, therefore the first-order conditions are necessary and sufficient for maximum. Therefore, the optimal insurance is (the unique if $U(\cdot)$ is strictly concave) solution to:

$$(1 - q)u'(w - x) = q(r - 1)u'(w + (r - 1)x - D).$$

We will call insurance actuarially fair if $r = 1/q$ (that is the firm breaks even on average). Then $q(r - 1) = 1 - q$ and,

$$u'(w - x) = u'(w + (r - 1)x - D).$$

Let $u(\cdot)$ be strictly concave. Then, since $u'(\cdot)$ is strictly decreasing

$$w - x = w + (r - 1)x - D$$
$$x = D/r = qD.$$

Note that it leaves the customer with the same wealth $w - qD$ no matter whether the accident happened: a risk-averse individual insures fully if the price of insurance is actuarially fair.

5.4 Stochastic dominance

If we know an individual's Bernoulli utility then we can compare any two lotteries from her point of view. Now I am going to ask: given two monetary lotteries, under what conditions will I be able to say that any (risk-averse) individual prefers one to second, provided she prefers more to less.

Definition 2. Lottery $L_1 = (x_1, p_1; \ldots; x_n, p_n)$ is said to first-order stochastically dominate (FOSD) lottery $L_2 = (x_1, q_1; \ldots; x_n, q_n)$ if for any increasing Bernoulli utility function $u(\cdot)$

$$\sum_{i=1}^{n} p_i u(x_i) \geq \sum_{i=1}^{n} q_i u(x_i).$$

Our next objective is to derive a criterion, which will allow us to decide whether one lottery FOSD the other.

Definition 3. Function $F(\cdot)$ defined by

$$F(z) = \Pr(x < z)$$

is called a cumulative distribution function for random variable x.

Let $L = x = (x_1, p_1; \ldots; x_n, p_n)$ and assume without loss of generality that $x_1 < x_2 < \cdots < x_n$. Then,

$$F(z) = 0, \quad \text{for } z < x_1,$$

$$F_L(z) = \sum_{i=1}^{k} p_i, \quad \text{for } x_k < z \leq x_{k+1},$$

$$F(z) = 1, \quad \text{for } z \geq x_n.$$

L_1 FOSD L_2 iff $F_{L_1}(z) \leq F_{L_2}(z)$, that is the probability that the outcome is lower than any fixed level is smaller for lottery L_1.

Example 4. $L_1 = (0, 1/6; 1, 1/3; 2, 1/2)$ and $L_2 = (0, 1/3; 1, 1/3; 2, 1/3)$. Then L_1 FOSD L_2. Let us first establish it using the definition. We have to check that,

$$\frac{1}{6}u(0) + \frac{1}{3}u(1) + \frac{1}{2}u(2) \geq \frac{1}{3}u(0) + \frac{1}{3}u(1) + \frac{1}{3}u(2) \qquad (5.6)$$

for any increasing $u(\cdot)$. But inequality FOSD is equivalent to:

$$u(2) \geq u(0).$$

Definition 5. Let lotteries L_1 and L_2 have the same expected value (mean). Lottery $L_1 = (x_1, p_1; \ldots; x_n, p_n)$ is said to second-order stochastically dominate (SOSD) lottery $L_2 = (x_1, q_1; \ldots; x_n, q_n)$ if for any increasing concave Bernoulli utility function $u(\cdot)$

$$\sum_{i=1}^{n} p_i u(x_i) \geq \sum_{i=1}^{n} q_i u(x_i).$$

Our next objective is to derive a criterion, which will allow us to decide whether one lottery SOSD the other.

Definition 6. A lottery L_2 is said to be obtained from lottery L_1 by a mean-preserving increase of risk if it is obtained by replacing an outcome x_i in lottery L_1 by a lottery with mean x_i.

Example 7. Let $L_1 = (0, 1/3; 1, 1/3; 2, 1/3)$ and $L_2 = (0, 1/2; 2, 1/2)$. Lottery L_2 is obtained from L_1 by replacing the outcome 1 with a lottery $(0, 1/2; 2, 1/2)$. For example, L_1 may be realized as: through a dice, if $\{1, 2\}$ get nothing, if $\{3, 4\}$ get one, if $\{5, 6\}$ get 2. L_2 provides the same payoff if the outcomes are $\{1, 2, 5, 6\}$ if the outcome is 3 or 4, through a coin and get nothing if H and two if T.

Distribution L_1 SOSD L_2 iff L_2 is obtained from lottery L_1 by a mean-preserving increase of risk. Intuitively L_2 contains more risk, since a certain outcome was replaced by the lottery. Therefore, any risk-averse individual will prefer L_1 to L_2.

Theory of general equilibrium developed above can be generalized for the situation characterized by uncertainty. The key to this generalization is concept of *contingent commodity*. In this approach, one models uncertainty as a possible realization of many states of world, characterized by a probability distribution and trades in promises to deliver a particular good in a particular state of the world, for example, deliver an umbrella if it is raining, deliver ice-cream if it is hot, etc. Such promises are known as contingent commodities. You will become acquainted with them if you take a more advanced course or go through suggested reading in the end of this part.

5.5 Problems

(1) Consider two lotteries,

$$L_1 = (x; p) = (0, 0.5; 1, 0.5),$$
$$L_2 = (y; q) = (0.09, 0.3; 0.25, 0.5; 1, 0.2).$$

Consider three individuals Ann, Bob, and Carol with utility functions:

1. $u(x) = \sqrt{x}$,
2. $u(x) = x$,
3. $u(x) = x^2$,

respectively. For every individual and every lottery, compute the certainty equivalent.

(2) Consider an individual with utility function:

$$u(x; \phi) = \frac{1 - \exp(-\phi x)}{\phi}. \tag{5.7}$$

(a) Compute the Arrow–Pratt coefficient of absolute risk aversion defined as:

$$r_A = -\frac{u''(x)}{u'(x)}. \tag{5.8}$$

(b)* Verify directly that,

$$\lim_{\phi \to 0} u(x; \phi) = x. \tag{5.9}$$

(c)* Assume individual considers buying a lottery with payoffs that are normally distributed with mean μ and variance σ^2. Compute the certainty equivalent.

Bibliographic notes

The material of this chapter constitutes the oldest part of mathematical economics. Debreu (1959) established conditions for the existence of a utility function and established existence of economic equilibrium from the first principles. By that time mathematical economics was in a stage of rapid development for more than a decade. For example, von Neumann and Morgenstern (1944) established expected utility representation of preferences over lotteries. Arrow and Debreu (1954) established existence of an equilibrium for a competitive economy allowing for uncertainty. Compared to earlier models, the Arrow–Debreu model radically generalized the notion of a commodity, differentiating commodities by time and place of delivery. They achieved it by introducing a concept of *contingent commodity* and therefore treating "oranges in Boston today" and "oranges in Chicago in a week" as distinct commodities. The Arrow–Debreu model applies to economies with maximally complete markets, in which there exists a market for every time period and forward prices for every commodity at all time periods and in all places.

By now there are good textbook treatments of these topics. To those readers who would like to familiarize themselves with this material on graduate level, we recommend Mas-Colell *et al.* (1995).

However, no sooner than the theory of expected utility was formulated, it came under attack from experimental economists and psychologists who have uncovered a growing body of evidence that individuals do not necessarily conform to many of the key assumptions or predictions of the subjective expected utility model of choice under uncertainty, and seem to depart from this model in systematic and predictable ways. Two responses to these critiques were considered in the literature. The first response is to consider alternative models of preferences; the second is to allow for a wedge between preferences and choices. It should be mentioned that these approaches are not mutually exclusive. For detailed discussion of the literature that grew out of these responses, see Basov (2016).

References

K. J. Arrow and G. Debreu, Existence of an equilibrium for a competitive economy, *Econometrica* **22**: 265–290, 1954.

S. Basov, *Bounded Rationality, Social Norms, and Optimal Contracts*, Springer-Verlag, Berlin, Germany, 2016.

G. Debreu, *Theory of Value: An Axiomatic Analysis of Economic Equilibrium.* Yale University Press, New Haven, CT, USA, 1959.

A. Mas-Colell, M. D. Whinston and J. R. Green, *Microeconomic Theory*, Oxford University Press, Oxford, UK, 1995.

J. von Neumann and O. Morgenstern, *Theory of Games and Economic Behavior,* Princeton University Press, Princeton, NJ, USA, 1944.

PART III
Strategic Interactions

Overview

So far, we assumed that individuals respond to market prices but do not have to take into account actions of each other directly. This assumption, however, is not satisfied when a small number of economic actors are locked in a strategic interaction. An example of such an interaction is an oligopolistic market, where the firms have to predict production and pricing decisions of each other to be able to devise a rational course of action. The study of such situations is the subject of game theory.

Chapter 6

Game Theory

Game theory is the main mathematical tool to model strategic interactions in economics and other social sciences. In economics, we assume that individuals are rational and try to predict consciously the actions of their opponents and best respond to them. An alternative approach, *evolutionary game theory*, originated in biology. Under this approach, each individual is characterized by a strategy and the rate of replication of individuals in increasing the success of their strategy. We will not discuss evolutionary game theory in this book, but some references will be provided in the end of this part.

6.1 What is a game

You probably know many different games. Among them are board games: chess, checkers, backgammon, monopoly; sports such as soccer, basketball, hockey, and many others. To describe a game in general, one has to first specify players, for example, Karpov and Kasparov in the world chess championship or Brazil versus Germany in a soccer World Cup final. One has to also specify a set of rules. They are easier described in chess then in soccer, but in both cases they exist. Outcomes specify what will happen under different circumstances. For example, certain chess positions are known as checkmate and stalemate, and when the ball in soccer crosses the goal line it is a goal. Finally, one has to specify payoffs corresponding to outcomes. If a chess game ends in stalemate each player gets a point, if in a checkmate the delivering player gets a point and the receiving player zero points. We will assume that the payoffs are given in terms of Bernoulli utilities.

6.2 The normal form and the extensive form

The *extensive* form of a game explicitly specifies the order of actions. Formally, a game in an extensive form consists of:

(1) A set of nodes, X, set of actions, A, and set of players $I = \{1, \ldots, I\}$.
(2) Function $p : X \rightarrow X \cup \varnothing$, specifying the immediate predecessor, $p(x) \neq \varnothing$ for all nodes but one, called the *initial* node. Correspondence $s :$ $X \rightarrow X \cup \varnothing$ called immediate successor and defined by $s(x) = p^{-1}(x)$ (that is $p(s(x)) = x$). If $s(x) = \varnothing$, the node is called terminal. Iterating $p(x)$ and $s(x)$ we find all predecessors and all successors of node x. No node is both a predecessor and a successor of node x.
(3) The set of actions available at any non-terminal node.
(4) The partition of nodes into information sets. If a player is within an information set, she cannot distinguish between the nodes that belong to this set. In particular, the set of actions available at any node of an information set should be the same.
(5) Assignment to each information set a player (or Nature) who moves at it.
(6) If the Nature controls an information set, one should assign the set of probabilities with which each possible choice is made.
(7) In each terminal node, payoffs to each player are specified in terms of their Bernoulli utilities.

An important notion is that of a strategy. Intuitively, a strategy is a fully contingent plan of actions. Suppose you would like to send your agent to play the game for you. For example, if you are a prime minister, you might want your ambassador to conduct the trade negotiations. In that case, you might want to provide her with a fully contingent plan of how to behave in response to different proposals.

Formally, a pure strategy of player i is a rule that assigns to each information set controlled by player i an action available at this set. Note: actions should be specified even at information sets that will not be reached due to the previous actions of player i.

The *normal* form of a game specifies the set of players, their strategies, and payoffs that correspond to each strategy profile. One can always move from an extensive form to a normal, but the important information about timing (or rather the information available at the time of the move) will be lost. On the other hand, one can move from the normal form to the extensive if one is willing to make assumptions about the timing (e.g., all the moves are made simultaneously).

6.3 Mixed strategies and behavioral strategies

I have introduced above, a notion of a pure strategy. Sometimes, however, a player might wish to randomize her choice. For example, the prisoner might select to flip a coin and confess iff it comes H. Such a strategy is called a mixed strategy. Formally, a mixed strategy is a probability distribution on the set of the pure strategies. We will see later, that sometimes the players will choose to randomize their choices to keep opponents from guessing.

If we have an extensive form game, we can capture the idea of randomization in two different ways:

(1) Write a corresponding normal form game and allow for the mixed strategies.
(2) Consider randomized actions at each information set.

The latter procedure gives rise to *behavioral* strategies. It is clear that to each behavioral strategy corresponds a mixed strategy. Can any mixed strategy be represented as a behavioral strategy? It turns out that the answer is YES, as long as the players have a perfect recall: that is the player does not forget what she knew.

6.4 Simultaneous-move games of complete information

In this section, I assume that the players have complete information, i.e., the normal form of the game is known to all players.

6.4.1 *Dominant and dominated strategies*

Consider a game $\Gamma = \{I, \{S_i\}, u_i\}$ where I is the set of players, S_i is a set of strategies of player i and u_i is her Bernoulli utility. Let s_{-i} denote a strategy profile of all players expect for player i and S_{-i} set of all possible strategy profiles for the players other than i.

Definition 1. A strategy $s_i \in S_i$ is called a strictly dominant strategy if for all $s_i' \in S_i$, $s_i' \neq s_i$

$$u_i(s_i, s_{-i}) > u_i(s_i', s_{-i}) \quad \forall s - i \in S_{-i}.$$

In words, there exists no other strategy that performs at least as good as s_i, no matter what the others do.

Definition 2. A strategy $s_i \in S_i$ is called strictly dominated if $\exists s_i' \in S_i$, $s_i' \neq s_i$

$$u_i(s_i', s_{-i}) > u_i(s_i, s_{-i}) \quad \forall s_{-i} \in S_{-i}.$$

In words, there exists another strategy that performs better than s_i no matter what the others do. No rational player will ever play a strictly dominated strategy.

Definition 3. A strategy $s_i \in S_i$ is called weakly dominated if $\exists s_i' \in S_i$, $s_i' \neq s_i$

$$u_i(s_i', s_{-i}) \geq u_i(s_i, s_{-i}) \quad \forall s_{-i} \in S_{-i}.$$

In words, there exists another strategy that performs at least as good as s_i, no matter what the others do. It is quite reasonable to assume that the players will not play strictly dominated strategies. However, that statement is not as innocent as it sounds.

Iterated Deletion of the Strictly Dominated Strategies and Rationalizable Strategies and Common Knowledge of Rationality (CKR)

Consider the DA game.

	DC	C
DC	$0, -2$	$-8, -1$
C	$-1, -8$	$-5, -5$

Note that DC is a strictly dominated strategy for the column player. After it is eliminated, the row player faces a payoff matrix.

	C
DC	$-8, -1$
C	$-5, -5$

Now DC is strictly dominated and the result is (C, C). The process described is known as an iterated deletion of strictly dominant strategies. Note that for the row player not to play DC, he should not only be rational but also believe that the column player is rational and will not play DC. Under the CKR[1] assumption, this process can go indefinitely (for games with more strategies). Only the strategies that survive it may be played by the players who have CKR. Instead of eliminating strictly dominated strategies, one might have eliminated strategies that are never a best response to any mixed strategy of the rivals. This process is known as the elimination if the never best responses and the set of strategies that survive it is known as the set of rationalizable strategies. If $I = 2$, there is no difference between the set of the rationalizable strategies and the set of strategies that survive the iterated deletion of the strictly dominant strategies.

6.5 Nash equilibrium (NE)

Definition 4. A strategy profile $s = (s_1, \ldots, s_I)$ constitutes a NE if

$$u_i(s_i, s_{-i}) \geq u_i(s_i', s_{-i}) \quad \forall s_i' \in S_i.$$

In words, a strategy profile is a NE if unilateral deviation is not optimal for any player. Of course, if all players have strictly dominating strategy (e.g., prisoners' dilemma), then the NE exists and is unique. NE never contains a strictly dominated strategy but it may contain a weakly dominated strategy.

6.6 Simultaneous-move games of incomplete information

A game is called a game of *perfect* information if all information sets are singletons. An example of such a game is chess: a player knows exactly all the position. Of course, all simultaneous-move games are games of imperfect information. So are most card games.

---

[1]CKR means that players are rational, know that other players are rational, know that other players know they are rational, and so on, till infinity.

A conceptually different concept, is a game of complete information. A game is a game of *complete* information if each player knows the game tree (or the payoff matrix for the simultaneous-move game). All games we considered so far are the games of complete information. However, it is easy to come up with economically relevant examples when the last assumption is violated. Consider, for example, the first-price sealed bid auction. Two players bid for an object. Valuation of the first bidder is v_1 and the valuation to the second bidder is v_2. Each player submits a bid $b_i \geq 0$. Player with the highest bid wins the object and pays her bid. If they tie, the allocation is determined by the toss of a fair coin. The expected utility of player i who submits bid b_i is:

$$u_i(b_i) = (v_i - b_i)\theta(b_i - b_j),$$

where,

$$\theta(b_i - b_j) = \begin{cases} 1 & \text{if } b_i > b_j, \\ 1/2 & \text{if } b_i = b_j, \\ 0 & \text{if } b_i < b_j. \end{cases}$$

Since b_i may in general take infinitely many values, the payoff matrix will be infinitely dimensional. However, if we assume that b_i is allowed to take only finitely many values, we can draw it. For example, if rules are such that $b_i \in \{1, 2\}$, the matrix has a form:

	1	2
1	$1/2(v_1 - 1), 1/2(v_2 - 1)$	$0, v_2 - 2$
2	$v_1 - 2, 0$	$1/2(v_1 - 2), 1/2(v_2 - 2)$

If the valuations were public knowledge, this would be a game of complete information. However, in reality it is rarely the case. Usually, v_i are private information. Therefore, neither player knows the payoff matrix and the game is a game of incomplete information.

6.6.1 *Harsanyi doctrine*

Note that all solution concepts we developed in the previous lecture do not work for the games of incomplete information. To overcome this difficulty, Harsanyi proposed to look at such games from a different perspective, which will reduce them to the games of imperfect information.

Consider the auction example above and assume that at time zero both players do not know their own valuations as well as the valuations of their opponents. Then chance moves and distributes types with some probabilities (in the above example, it may select independently valuations of the bidders from a set $V = \{v^1, \ldots, v^n\}$ with respective probabilities $p_1, \ldots, p_n$. Both, set V and the probabilities are common knowledge. At time $t = 1$, each player observes their valuation). In general, I will refer to the private information a player has as her type. In the preceding example, type of the player is her valuation. At time zero, each player devises a fully contingent plan of how to behave for every realization of her type. This trick reduces a game with incomplete information to the game of imperfect information. The price you have to pay is that the notion of a strategy is becoming more complicated. Now the strategy is not simply an action you were going to take after your type is realized but *a function from the type space into the action space*. For example, a strategy in the first-price auction is a bidding function, which states how much you will bid for any possible valuation, rather than just your actual bid. A NE in the game so defined is called Bayesian Nash Equilibrium.

6.7 Dynamic games

In the previous lecture, we considered the simultaneous move games and developed equilibrium concepts for them. This equilibrium concept, NE, is based on the normal form representation of the game. Often the games have an explicit temporal structure. To take it explicitly into account, we need to develop some new concepts.

6.7.1 *Subgames and SPNE*

Definition 5. A subgame of an extensive form game is a subset of the game having the following properties:

(i) It begins in a singleton information set, i.e., the information set containing a single decision node, and contains all the successors of this node.
(ii) If a decision node belongs to a subgame, the information set that contains it also belongs to the subgame.

One example of a subgame is, of course, the game itself. Simultaneous move games, considered in the previous lecture have no other subgames. Any subgame, different from the game itself is called a proper subgame.

Definition 6. A strategy profile is a subgame perfect nash equilibrium (SPNE) if its restriction to any subgame is a NE in that subgame.

Example 7. Suppose a potential entrant decides whether to enter the market. If she stays out she gets a payoff of zero, while the incumbent earns the payoff of two. If she decides to enter, both firms have to decide simultaneously whether to fight or accommodate, i.e., the entrance decision is followed by a game (E controls the raws):

	A	F
A	$3, 1$	$-2, -1$
F	$1, -2$	$-3, -1$

Note that the game shown in the table is a subgame of the original game. The only NE in this game is (A, A) (in fact, (A, A) can be obtained by iterated deletion of the strictly dominated strategies). Therefore, in any SPNE the incumbent should play A and part of the entrant's strategy should be A if In. To see, whether E should play In or Out replace the post entry game with its NE payoff $(3, 1)$. Then, clearly E should play In. Therefore, the only SPNE is $(In, A$ if $In; A)$. Note that the game has other NE, for example, $(Out, F$ if $In, F)$.

6.7.2 *Backward induction (BI) and CKR*

The process we used to solve the previous two examples is known as the backward induction. It works as follows:

(1) Start at the end of the game tree, identify all the subgames that do not have proper subgames and find all their NE.
(2) Select one NE in each game and replace it with the equilibrium payoffs.
(3) Repeat steps 1 and 2 until you reach the root of the tree.
(4) If on step 1 multiple NE were found, repeat all the procedure with the different NE.

All SPNE can be found using the BI. Consider a special case, when the game is perfect information, i.e., all the information sets are singletons. In that case, BI suggests that one should start considering the players that control the next to the terminal nodes and determine their decisions. Then replace those nodes by the payoffs and move backwards until the root of the game tree is reached. If there are no ties in any player's payoffs, then the outcome of this process is unique. Therefore, the games of perfect information in which payoffs of each player in all terminal nodes are different have a unique SPNE. Note that in perfect information game, BI is equivalent to CKR.

6.7.3 *Some critique of the BI*

Consider the following game:

(1) Player one can move L or R. If she moves R, the game is finished and the payoffs are $(1, 100)$. If she moves left, go to step 2.
(2) Player two can move ℓ or r. If she moves r the payoffs are $(2, 1)$, if she moves ℓ they are $(-100, 0)$.

The only SPNE is (L, r), but is it a really good idea for player one to move L?

The Centipede Game

This game was invented by Robert W. Rosenthal in 1981 and was used in numerous experiments to illustrate some difficulties with SPNE as a predictive tool.

(1) Player one can stop a game of pass. If she stops, payoffs are $(1, 1)$ if she passes, the game continues.
(2) Now player two can stop or pass. If she stops, payoffs are $(0, 3)$ if she passes, the game continues.

Note that if you pass and your opponent stops, you lose one and she gains two. After a 100 decision nodes, the game finally finishes. At the last move of player, one she decides between stopping (payoffs are $(99, 99)$) or passing, in which case player, two decides whether to stop with payoffs $(98, 101)$ or pass with payoffs $(100, 100)$. Note that at her last move, player two will stop ($101 > 100$), predicting this player one should stop a move before ($99 > 98$). Reasoning in this way, we see that the only SPNE is ($stop, stop, \ldots, stop$; $stop, stop, \ldots, stop$) (a reminder, a strategy should say what you do in each node. In this game, each player controls 50 nodes and has two choices at each, so each player has $2^{50} \approx 10^{15}$ strategies). The outcome is $(1, 1)$. However, it seems a rather counter-intuitive prediction. In real experiments, the players reach the middle of the tree.

6.7.4   *Weak perfect Bayesian equilibrium (WPBE)*

The basic idea for formulating the notion of WPBE is that of *sequential rationality*. It requires that the choice of action at each information set is supported by some system of beliefs. A system of beliefs at the information set is simply an assignment of probabilities to each node of the information set. Formally, a strategy profile $(\sigma_1, \ldots, \sigma_I)$ is sequentially rational at information set H controlled by player i, given a system of beliefs $\mu(x|H)$ if,

$$E(u_i(\sigma_i, \sigma_{-i})|H, \mu, \sigma) \geq E(u_i(\sigma_i, \sigma_{-i})|H, \mu, \sigma'_i, \sigma_i). \qquad (6.1)$$

A strategy profile and a system of beliefs constitute a WPBE if the strategy profile is sequentially rational and the beliefs are consistent with the strategies used.

To see what consistent means, suppose the mixed strategy profile used by the players is σ and let $P_\sigma(H)$ be the probability of reaching the information set H under σ and $P_\sigma(x)$ be the probability of reaching decision node x. Let $x \in H$. According to the Bayes' rule, the conditional probability $P_\sigma(x|H)$ is given by:

$$P_\sigma(x|H) = \frac{P_\sigma(H|x)P_\sigma(x)}{P_\sigma(H)}. \qquad (6.2)$$

$P_\sigma(H|x) = 1$, since $x \in H$ therefore,

$$P_\sigma(x|H) = \frac{P_\sigma(x)}{P_\sigma(H)}. \qquad (6.3)$$

Let $\mu(x|H)$ be the belief of the player that she is at decision node x, conditional on her knowing that she is at information set H. Then the beliefs are consistent with the strategies used by the players if:

$$\mu(x|H) = P_\sigma(x|H). \qquad (6.4)$$

6.8 Problems

(1) Find all NE (in pure and mixed strategies) in the following game

	A	B	C
a	1,1	0,2	4,4
b	0,1	3,0	2,2
c	2,3	0,0	5,−1

(2) Consider the following situation, describing an absent minded driver. The driver has to take the second turn right. Unfortunately, she does not remember whether she has already passed a crossroad. Obviously, this game does not have perfect recall.

(a) Identify all pure, mixed, and behavioral strategies.
(b) Give an example of a mixed strategy in this game that cannot be realized as a behavioral strategy.

(3) Consider the following game. The row player believes that with probability μ the column player has the preferences summarized by the top table and with probability $1 - \mu$ has preferences summarized by the bottom table. Find the Bayes–Nash equilibrium of the game.

	D	C
D	0,−2	−8,−1
C	−1,−8	−5,−5

	D	C
D	0,−2	−8,−7
C	−1,−8	−5,−11

Chapter 7

Theory of Imperfect Competition and Industry Structure

In this chapter, I will introduce theory of industry structure. So far we considered a model where firms were competitive and number of the competitors was fixed. We developed equilibrium concept to describe such a situation: Walrasian equilibrium. I will start this chapter by describing the situation, where firm are competitive, but their number is not fixed, since there is a possibility of entry. We will see that one has to develop a new equilibrium notion: a long-run equilibrium with entry, where to the condition of equality of demand and supply that determines equilibrium prices the = zero profit condition, that determines the equilibrium number of firms is added. Then I am going to relax the assumption that firms are competitive, which will lead us to the theory of imperfect competition.

7.1 A competitive firm

A competitive firm takes the market price as given and chooses its production level to maximize profits, i.e., a competitive firm solves:

$$\max(R(q) - C(q)), \tag{7.1}$$

where $R(q)$ is the firm's revenue, given by:

$$R(q) = pq \tag{7.2}$$

and p is the market price, taken as given by the firm. The first-order condition is:

$$C'(q) = p, \tag{7.3}$$

where $'$ denotes derivative. Recall that the derivative of the cost function is known as the *marginal cost* and is denoted $MC(q)$. A competitive firm produces at the point, where price equals marginal cost. For example, if

$$C(q) = F + \frac{q^2}{2}, \tag{7.4}$$

where F is the fixed cost, then $MC(q) = C'(q) = q$ and the firm's *supply function* is:

$$q_c = p, \tag{7.5}$$

provided price p is large enough that the firm makes non-negative profits. The firm's profit will be:

$$\pi_c = pq_c - C(q) = \frac{p^2}{2} - F. \tag{7.6}$$

Therefore, the firm's *supply function* is:

$$q_c = \begin{cases} p & \text{if } p \le \sqrt{2F}, \\ 0 & \text{otherwise.} \end{cases} \tag{7.7}$$

If one assumes free entry, the price and the number of firms, n, can be determined if one knows the market demand, by equating it with total supply nq_c and requiring that the profits per firm should be zero. This condition is known as a *zero profit condition*. Note that zero profit condition refers to economic profits. Accounting profits may still be positive.

For an example of using the zero profit condition **n**, assume that a competitive industry in which firms are described by (7.1)–(7.6) faces demand

$$Q^d = 100 - p. \tag{7.8}$$

The equilibrium price in an economy with n firms can be found from:

$$np = 100 - p \Leftrightarrow p = \frac{100}{n+1}, \tag{7.9}$$

which implies that a firm's profits are:

$$\pi_c = \frac{10,000}{2(n+1)^2} - F. \tag{7.10}$$

Equating profits to zero, one obtains:

$$n = \frac{100}{\sqrt{2F}} - 1. \tag{7.11}$$

(Strictly speaking, n is the biggest integer smaller than RHS of the above expression, but ignore that for a moment.) If, for example, $F = 12.5$, then $n = 19$, which allows us to calculate $p = 5$, and the total quantity sold on the market is $Q = 95$, where each firm produces $q = 5$.

7.2 A monopoly

A monopolist will take into account that amount it produces will affect the price at which it will be able to sell the output. Suppose a firm has to choose the level of output to produce. Producing q units of output costs $C(q)$ and results in the revenue $R(q)$. The profit function is given by,

$$\pi(q) = R(q) - C(q). \tag{7.12}$$

The first-order conditions for optimization is:

$$R'(q) = C'(q), \tag{7.13}$$

or

$$\mathrm{MR}(q) = \mathrm{MC}(q), \tag{7.14}$$

where MR stands for marginal revenue $(\mathrm{MR}(q) = R'(q))$ and MC stands for marginal cost $(\mathrm{MC}(q) = c'(q))$. The cost function is determined by the technological capabilities of the firm, while the revenue function is determined by the market conditions. The revenue of a monopolist is:

$$R(q) = p(q) * q \tag{7.15}$$

and the first-order condition becomes

$$p'(q)q + p(q) = \mathrm{MC}(q), \tag{7.16}$$

or re-arranging:

$$p(q)\left(1 + \frac{1}{\eta}\right) = \mathrm{MC}(q), \tag{7.17}$$

where

$$\eta = \frac{q'(p)p}{q} = \frac{p(q)}{qp'(q)}, \tag{7.18}$$

is the elasticity of demand. Equation (7.17) implies that

$$1 + \frac{1}{\eta} > 0 \Longleftrightarrow \eta < -1, \tag{7.19}$$

i.e., the monopolist always produces at the elastic portion of the demand, i.e., at the point where $\eta < -1$. If demand is always inelastic (e.g., $q = p^{-\varepsilon}$,[1] with $\varepsilon < 1$), the market collapses since the monopolist has an incentive to decrease quantity and increase price without limit.

Consider a case when the cost function is linear, i.e.,

$$C(q) = cq. \tag{7.20}$$

In that case,

$$p\left(1 + \frac{1}{\eta}\right) = c. \tag{7.21}$$

Define the mark-up, m, charged by the monopolist by:

$$p = c(1 + m), \tag{7.22}$$

i.e., the mark-up is the fraction of price in excess of the MC. Combining Eqs. (7.21) and (7.22), one obtains:

$$m = -\frac{1}{1 + \eta}. \tag{7.23}$$

Since the monopolist always produces in the elastic part of the demand curve ($\eta < -1$), the markup is always positive. As the demand becomes more elastic (as the absolute value of η increases), the mark-up decreases. Intuitively, as the consumers become more sensitive to price, the monopolist becomes less willing to charge high price for the good. On the other hand, as the elasticity approaches -1, the mark-up converges to infinity. Note that since the monopolist's decision determines both the quantity and the price, one cannot speak of a supply curve for the monopolist.

---

[1] For this demand function $\eta = -\varepsilon$.

Let us assume that the demand is,

$$p(q) = a - bq \qquad (7.24)$$

for some positive a and b. Then,

$$R(q) = aq - bq^2 \Leftrightarrow \mathrm{MR}(q) = a - 2bq \qquad (7.25)$$

and the monopolist's production level is found from:

$$a - 2bq_m = c \Leftrightarrow q_m = \frac{a-c}{2b}. \qquad (7.26)$$

Note that the monopolist will produce a positive quantity as long as $a > c$, otherwise the monopolist produces zero quantity and the market collapses. The corresponding price is,

$$p_m = a - bq_m = \frac{a+c}{2} \qquad (7.27)$$

which is greater than c as long as $a > c$, i.e., as long as the monopolist chooses to produce. The monopolist's profits are:

$$\pi_m = (p_m - c)q_m = \frac{(a-c)^2}{4b}. \qquad (7.28)$$

File Chapter_6.xlsx (Available at: http://www.worldscientific.com/world scibooks/10.1142/10138) provides an example of creating a spreadsheet to solve the monopoly problem with constant marginal cost, c, and inverse demand function:

$$p(q) = b\exp(-\alpha q). \qquad (7.29)$$

Note that if $c > b$, then the optimal production level is zero, i.e., the monopoly stays out of the market. Otherwise, there exists unique optimal solution which can be found using the spreadsheet, where monopoly profits are programed in the target cell, D6, and quantity is in the changing cell B5. Monopoly price is computed in the cell D7.

7.3 Oligopoly

Oligopoly describes the situation when there is more than one firm on the market, but the number of firms is sufficiently small, so that each firm thinks strategically about the decisions of their rivals. The outcome of such competition strongly depends on whether firms compete in price or in quantity. For a discussion of conditions under which price or quantity competition best describes the situation in the industry, Price competition best describes the situation when goods are easy to produce at demand, while quantity competition is the best description when the firms have to commit to some production capacity. In this section, I am going to assume that $C(q) = cq$, i.e., that the marginal cost is constant.

7.3.1 *Bertrand competition*

First, let us assume that there are just two firms on the market and they compete in price (the so-called *Bertrand* competition) and let the firms have the same marginal cost, c. The customers demand at most one unit of good each and have valuation for this unit, which is higher than production cost.

We will argue that in that case, both firms charge marginal cost and split the market. Let firm 1 charge $p_1 > c$, then firm 2 will charge p_2 just below p_1 (but still above c), steal all the customers from firm 1 and earn positive profits; of course, now firm 1 will undercut firm 2, and this will continue until both firms charge $p = c$ and earn zero profits. Hence, with price competition, the market reproduces the competitive outcome with just two firms. Obviously, result still holds if there are more than two firms.

What if firms have different marginal costs. Let us assume without loss of generality that there are n firms on the market and firms are ordered in such a way that $c_1 \leq c_2 \leq \cdots \leq c_n$. We claim that in that case, the equilibrium price will be c_2 and firm one serve the entire market as long as $c_1 < c_2$ and split the market with $k - 1$ other firms if $c_1 = c_2 = \cdots = c_k < c_{k+1}$. Indeed, if price is above c_2, firms 1 and 2 will have incentive to undercut and steal business from the competitors. If price is exactly c_2, firm 1 will have incentive to undercut by an infinitesimal amount to steal all business from firm 2. However, it will have no further incentive to undercut, since there are no other firms who are willing to steal business at this price. Note that in this case, the most efficient firm earns positive profits determined by its cost advantage over the next most efficient competitor.

7.3.2 *Cournot competition*

Effects of competition are less drastic if the firms compete in quantity (the so-called *Cournot* competition). Suppose there are n identical firms and let us assume that the inverse market demand is given by:

$$p(q) = a - bQ, \qquad (7.30)$$

where

$$Q = \sum_{i-1}^{n} q_i, \tag{7.31}$$

and q_i is the level of production of firm i. Let

$$Q_{-i} = Q - q_i, \tag{7.32}$$

be the total production of all firms other than i. Firm i chooses q_i to solve

$$\max((a - b(Q_{-i} + q_i))q_i - cq_i). \tag{7.33}$$

When performing the maximization, it takes Q_{-i} as given. The first-order condition is:

$$a - bQ_{-i} - c - 2bq_i = 0. \tag{7.34}$$

Repeating it for all firms, one gets a system of n linear equation in n unknowns. Such a system has a unique solution. Since all firms are identical, at the solution $q_i = q$ for all firms, therefore $Q_{-i} = (n-1)q$ and (7.34) implies:

$$q = \frac{a - c}{(n+1)b} \Rightarrow Q = \frac{n(a - c)}{(n+1)b}. \tag{7.35}$$

Note that though the output per firm decreases with the number of the competitors, the industry output increases and as n converges to infinity and approaches the competitive level,

$$Q_c = \frac{a - c}{b}. \tag{7.36}$$

The market price is,

$$p = a - bQ = \frac{a + nc}{n + 1}, \tag{7.37}$$

and as n converges to infinity, it approaches the competitive price $p = c$. The profits per firm are

$$\pi = (p - c)q = \frac{(a - c)^2}{(n + 1)^2 b}, \tag{7.38}$$

and industry profits are

$$\pi^I = \frac{n(a - c)^2}{(n + 1)^2 b} = \frac{4n}{(n + 1)^2}\pi_m. \tag{7.39}$$

Note that for any $n > 1$, the industry profits are below the monopoly's profits, they decrease in n and approach zero as $n \to \infty$, i.e., competition increases aggregate production and decreases the industry profits, to the benefit of the consumers.

This analysis shows that there are three factors determining performance of an industry. First, *production technology*, which manifests itself in the conditional cost function $c(q)$. It can be affected by the firm through R&D. Second, the performance if affected by the *demand factors,* which in the models in this section are summarized by parameters a and b (one can imagine more complicated demand functions with more parameters). Firms may have limited control over them through advertising campaigns, but should largely take them as given. Finally, performance is affected by the *competitiveness of the market*. An innovative firm may enjoy for a while a (deserved) monopolists position on the market. However, a firm or an industry may also seek to limit competition through socially costly rent-seeking (e.g., lobbying the government for trade tariffs).

This analysis also sheds light on five forces described in the beginning of this part. Profitability and pricing are driven by the intensity of existing competition (think of number n of firms in the market in the Cournot model) and the basis on which it occurs (compare quantity and price competition). Competition is especially destructive to profitability if it gravitates solely to price competition, which effectively transfers profits from an industry to its customers. However, from the social point of view price competition is preferable, since it results in a competitive outcome, which maximizes social welfare. Role of customers is captured via the demand function. The more elastic demand (the more price sensitive are the customers) the smaller the mark-ups the firms can charge. Behavior of supplier can affect the cost of production, for example, via costs of raw materials, and therefore affect both equilibrium prices and profit margins. We have seen in the formal models that the number of firms can affect prices and profits (recall Cournot competition). However, even the threat of entry can affect behavior of incumbent firms, who can charge lower prices than they would otherwise to make entry unattractive. Existence of substitute products can make demand more elastic pushing down both profits and the equilibrium price.

The analysis also suggests that firms will try to spot niches in which they can enjoy monopoly position for a while. For example, if a firm develops a new product, then for a couple of periods, it could enjoy monopoly position and monopoly profits. It also explains industry life cycle, where an industry may start having just one firm enjoying monopoly profits, being gradually joined by rivals, at which stage profits fall and eventually reach the steady state level.

Cournot Oligopoly with Asymmetric Nonlinear Costs

Consider a Cournot game, but assume that marginal costs are linearly increasing in the level of production and differ across firms, i.e., the cost of production of firm i is

$$C_i(q) = \frac{c_i q_i^2}{2}. \tag{7.40}$$

Then the profit of firm i will be given by

$$\pi_i(q) = (a - b(Q_{-i} + q_i))q_i - \frac{c_i q_i^2}{2}. \tag{7.41}$$

The first-order condition is

$$bQ_{-i} + (2b + c_i)q_i = a. \tag{7.42}$$

Let us first consider the case $n = 2$. In that case, the output levels of the firms could be found by solving the following system of linear equations:

$$\begin{cases} (2b + c_1)q_1 + bq_2 = a, \\ bq_1 + (2b + c_2)q_2 = a. \end{cases} \tag{7.43}$$

It is easy to see that the unique solution is given by

$$\begin{cases} q_1 = \frac{a(b+c_2)}{\Delta}, \\ q_2 = \frac{a(b+c_1)}{\Delta}, \end{cases} \tag{7.44}$$

where

$$\Delta = c_1 c_2 + 3b^2 + 2bc_1 + 2bc_2. \tag{7.45}$$

In general case, the equilibrium is described by a system of linear equations. However, unless number of firm, n, is small it may be quite time consuming to find the solution analytically. In that case, one can use Excel to analyze the solution. To see how, we have first to learn how to do matrix algebra in Excel. For this purpose, let us write system (7.42) using matrix notation[2] as

$$A\mathbf{q} = \mathbf{a}, \tag{7.46}$$

where matrix A is defined

$$A = \begin{matrix} (2b + c_1) & b & \dots & \dots & b \\ b & (2b + c_2) & \dots & \dots & b \\ \dots & \dots & \dots & \dots & \dots \\ \dots & \dots & \dots & \dots & \dots \\ b & \dots & \dots & \dots & (2b + c_n) \end{matrix} \tag{7.47}$$

i.e., its diagonal terms are $2b - c_i$, while all other terms are b, while $\mathbf{a}$ is a constant column,

$$\mathbf{a} = \begin{matrix} a \\ a \\ \dots \\ \dots \\ a \end{matrix} \tag{7.48}$$

Matrix Algebra in Excel and Analysis of Cournot Game

Recall that a matrix is a rectangular array of numbers. An MxN−matrix contains M rows and N columns. One can think of a row vector as a $1xN$−matrix and of a column vector, an $Mx1$−matrix. A matrix is called square if $M = N$. When putting matrices into Excel, the entries should occupy adjacent columns. To see how the matrix operations are performed in Excel, open file Chapter_6_matrix_algebra.xlsx (Available at: http://www.worldscientific.com/worldscibooks/10.1142/10138).

Sheet *Addition and subtraction of matrices* contains example of adding and subtracting matrices. You are given two 5×2 matrices A and B. Matrix A occupies cells from $A4$ to $B8$ and matrix B cells from $D4$ to $E8$. To find their sum (difference), first check that both matrices have the same dimensions, i.e., both M and N are the same. Otherwise, the operation is not defined. Once you are satisfied that the dimensions are correct, highlight an area for $A + B.(A - B)$ and program into cell (i, j) the formula $= a_{ij} + b_{ij}$. For example, if cells from $G4$ to $H8$ are reserved for sum $A + B$ program into cell $G4$ the sum $A4 + D4$, etc. A similar procedure applies

---

[2]See Mathematical Appendix for a review of matrix algebra.

for multiplication by a scalar. Note that matrix of any dimension can be multiplied by a scalar. See sheet *S-Multiplication* for details.

Multiplication of matrices is a little bit trickier procedure. First, recall that the multiplication of an $LxM-$matrix A and an $MxN-$matrix B yields an $LxN-$matrix AB. If the number of A's columns differs from the number of B's rows, then AB is not defined. To understand the procedure for finding the matrix product open sheet *MMult*. Find out the dimension of the product AB. Highlight an area for AB (in the example presented this is the area $A9:E10$). Type $= MMULT(A4:C5, E4:I6)$.[3] Finally, press $[Ctrl] + [Shift] + [Enter]$. To find a transpose of a matrix, start also with highlighting the area of proper dimension and then using command $= Transpose$(cells occupied by the matrix) and then finishing by pressing $[Ctrl] + [Shift] + [Enter]$. To find inverse start with highlighting the area of the same dimension as matrix you want to invert,[4] type $= MINVERSE$(cells occupied by the matrix) and then finishing by pressing $[Ctrl] + [Shift] + [Enter]$. For examples of transposition and inversion, see sheets *Transposition* and *Inverse*.

To apply these techniques to the analysis of the Cournot model, note that the solution to (7.46) can be written as

$$\mathbf{q} = A^{-1}\mathbf{a} \qquad (7.49)$$

or in Excel notation

$$\mathbf{q} = \mathbf{MMULT}(\mathbf{MINVERSE}(A), \mathbf{a}), \qquad (7.50)$$

where one has to substitute into (7.50) names of cells occupied by matrix A ($\mathbf{a}$) for A ($\mathbf{a}$) respectively.

Sheet *Cournot* contains an example with $n = 5$ firms, costs $c_k = k$, $b = 1$, $a = 10$. First, create cells that contain cost and demand parameters, so you can easily change them if necessary. Then construct matrix A according to (7.47). It occupies array $B12:F16$. Vector $\mathbf{a}$ occupies array $H12:H16$. It is important that cells in this arrays contain formulae rather than numbers. It makes it easy to change parameters and reanalyze the solution if necessary. Finally, array $A20:A24$ is reserved for the solution. Highlight it, type $= MMULT(MINVERSE(B12:F16), H12:H16)$ then finishing by pressing $[Ctrl] + [Shift] + [Enter]$.

---

[3]$A4:C6$ and $E4:I6$ are the cells occupied by matrices A and B, respectively.
[4]Note that the matrix must be square.

7.3.3 *Stackelberg model of duopoly*

In both Bertrand and Cournot model, the firms make their strategic decisions simultaneously. In Stackelberg model, on the other hand, one firm is designated as a leader, while the other is the follower. Similar to the Cournot model, the strategic variable is the quantity. Here, we will consider the case of just two firms and linear inverse demand,

$$p = a - bQ. \tag{7.51}$$

We assume that firm 1 chooses its level of production first, the second firm observe this level and choose its level of production in response. Therefore, the strategy set of firm 1 is R_+, i.e., non-negative real numbers, corresponding to the level of production. A strategy of firm 2, on the other hand is a function $q_2(\cdot) : R_+ \to R_+$, which specifies a level of production chosen by firm 2 in response to a given level of production, chosen by firm 1.

The solution concept we employ is SPNE. Recall that to find the SPNE, one has to employ backward induction. That is, assuming that firm 1 has chosen production level q_1, firm 2 will solve

$$\max_{q_2}[(a - bq_1 - bq_2 - c)q_2]. \tag{7.52}$$

Note that the objective function is strictly concave and therefore the first-order condition that is necessary and sufficient takes the form:

$$a - bq_1 - 2bq_2 = 0 \Rightarrow q_2 = \frac{a - c - bq_1}{2b}. \tag{7.53}$$

Firm 1, when choosing its level of production takes into account the optimal response of firm 2, therefore it solves

$$\max_{q_1}[(a - bq_1 - bq_2 - c)q_1] \\ \text{s.t. } q_2 = \frac{a-c-bq_1}{2b}. \tag{7.54}$$

Substituting the best response of firm 2 into the leader's objective after simple algebra one obtains

$$\max_{q_1} \frac{1}{2}[(a - c - bq_1)q_1] \Rightarrow q_1 = \frac{a - c}{2b}. \tag{7.55}$$

Using the optimal response of the follower, i.e., Eq. (7.53) one obtains

$$q_2 = \frac{a - c}{4b}. \tag{7.56}$$

Total level of production by the industry is:

$$Q = q_1 + q_2 = \frac{3(a - c)}{4b}. \tag{7.57}$$

7.4 Problems

(1) Assume the inverse demand for the product of an industry is

$$p = 10 - Q. \tag{7.58}$$

Production cost is

$$c(Q) = 2 + Q. \tag{7.59}$$

Find the level of production by

(a) A monopoly.
(b) A Stackelberg duopoly.
(c) A Cournot oligopoly with n firms. Find the value of n for which profits are zero.
(d) A competitive market with n firms. Find the value of n for which profits are zero.
(e) A Bertrand oligopoly.

(2) Assume the inverse demand for the product of an industry is

$$p = \frac{10}{Q^\varepsilon}. \tag{7.60}$$

for some $\varepsilon > 0$. Production cost is,

$$c(Q) = cQ. \tag{7.61}$$

Find the level of production and price charged by a monopoly. How does this price depend on ε? What is economic meaning of ε?

(3) Consider a Cournot oligopoly with asymmetric constant marginal costs. Show that equilibrium levels of production are given by

$$q_i = \frac{a - nc_i + \sum_{j \neq i} c_j}{n + 1}, \tag{7.62}$$

(assume that all RHSs of (7.62) are positive).

(4) Assume a firm has a production function

$$y = f(z_1, z_2) = z_1^{1/6} z_2^{1/3}$$

and the factor prices are $w_1 = w_2 = 1$.

(a) Find the conditional cost of the firm.

(b) Assume that the firm is a competitive firm and find the firm's supply correspondence.
(c) Now suppose that the firm is a monopoly and the market demand for its product is given by,

$$p = 1 - y.$$

Find the quantity the firm will produce and the price it will charge.

Bibliographic notes

Standard game theory covered in this part is by now well understood. For textbook treatments, see Osborne and Rubinstein (1994) or Fudenberg and Tirole (1991) for a more technical exposition. For applications to the theory of market structure, see Tirole (1988). Most recent developments in the field of the game theory take place in the area of evolutionary game theory. For an introduction, see Samuelson (1997). For a more recent review of the developments in the field, see Sandholm (2010).

References

D. Fudenberg and J. Tirole, *Game Theory*, MIT Press, Cambridge, MA, USA, 1991.

L. Samuelson, *Evolutionary Games and Equilibrium Selection*, MIT Press, Cambridge, MA, USA, 1997.

M. J. Osborne and A. Rubinstein, *A Course in Game Theory*, MIT Press, Cambridge, MA, USA, 1994.

W. H. Sandholm, *Population Games and Evolutionary Dynamics*, MIT Press, Cambridge, MA, USA, 2010.

J. Tirole, *The Theory of Industrial Organization*, MIT Press, Cambridge, MA, USA, 1988.

PART IV

The Economics of Information

Overview

In this part, we consider models where one of the parties possesses private information relevant for the contracting parties. The models of these type can be divided into two broad categories: the hidden information models (informational asymmetries exist prior to contracting) and hidden action models (the information is symmetric prior to contracting, but an asymmetry arises at the post-contracting stage).

Chapter 8

Hidden Information Models

In this chapter, we consider three groups of models: *the adverse selection models, the signaling models, and the screening models*. In adverse selection model, one of economic actors usually referred as an agent possesses private information about some characteristic affecting payoff of the other agent. For example, a worker may be privately informed about her ability or a used car salesman can be privately informed about the quality of her car. Given a market wage, relatively worse worker is more likely to take a job, since he may have a worse outside option; given a price you are willing to pay for a used car, an owner is more likely to sell, if the car is of low quality. Therefore, the name for this kind of phenomena, *adverse selection*. We will consider three different scenarios. Pure adverse selection models are models where no party can take any steps to credibly reveal private information. Signaling models are models where the informed party takes a step to reveal her private information, for example, used car salesman issuing a warranty. Screening models refer to situations where the uninformed party tries to devise a menu of contracts that will make the informed party to reveal their information. For example, dividing jobs into easy and complicated ones can force low ability type to opt for the easier job, since it will be too hard for them to deal with the complicated tasks and even higher pay will not be enough to compensate for the effort.

8.1 The adverse selection model

Assume a worker has two options: to work in the market or to work at home. Productivity of the worker at the market place is equal to her ability θ and is the private information of the worker. It is, however, CK that θ is distributed on $[\underline{\theta}, \overline{\theta}]$ according to the density $f(\cdot)$. Her productivity at home is $r(\theta)$. For any market wage, w, the set of workers that work at the market is

$$M(w) = \{\theta : r(\theta) \leq w\}.$$

Note that if $r(\cdot)$ is increasing (workers who are more productive at market are also more productive at home), only the least productive workers will work at the market. The expected productivity of the workers on the market is given by

$$Q(w) = E(\theta|r(\theta) \leq w) = \frac{1}{F(r^{-1}(w))} \int_{\underline{\theta}}^{r^{-1}(w)} \theta f(\theta)d\theta,$$

where $F(\cdot)$ is the cumulative distribution function of θ defined by

$$F(\theta) = \int_{\underline{\theta}}^{\theta} f(\beta)d\beta.$$

The equilibrium wage is defined from

$$Q(w) = w.$$

In adverse selection models, an equilibrium with a positive employment may fail to exist even if it is efficient for everyone to work at the market. Indeed, assume that θ is distributed uniformly on $[0, 1]$ (i.e., $f(\theta) = 1$ and $F(\theta) = \theta$) and,

$$r(\theta) = \frac{2}{3}\theta.$$

Since

$$r(\theta) \leq \theta$$

for all θ it is efficient for everyone to work at the market. But

$$Q(w) = \frac{2}{3w} \int_0^{\frac{3}{2}w} \theta d\theta = \frac{3}{4}w,$$

and the only equilibrium wage is

$$w = 0.$$

Nobody chooses to be employed at this wage.

8.2 The general signaling model

Suppose a competitive employer wants to hire a worker. The employers utility from hiring the worker is

$$u_E(\theta, w, s) = g(\theta, s) - w,$$

where θ is an *unobservable* worker's ability and w the wage paid to the worker. The worker can choose to send a signal s to the market at cost $c(s, \theta)$. Her utility is

$$u_W(\theta, w, s) = w - c(s, \theta).$$

Here, we assume that $c_\theta < 0$ (higher ability decreases the cost of signaling) and $c_{s\theta} \leq 0$ (higher ability decreases the marginal cost (MC) of signaling). Given the signal, the employers on the market forms beliefs about the worker's type. Then employers offer wages in a competitive way, i.e., the wage equals the expected productivity given the signal. Note that in signaling models the worker (the informed party) moves first. The relevant solution concept is Weak perfect Bayesian equilibrium (WPBE).

8.2.1 *The Spence model and economics of education*

In the Spence model, there are two types of workers, $\theta \in \{\theta_L, \theta_H\}$ and the signal is the workers education, so I will denote it e rather than s. The worker's type is interpreted as her ability and let us assume that the market productivity is equal to the workers type and does not depend on education. In this case, we will say that education is a pure signaling device. This assumption is made solely to simplify the exposition and concentrate on the signaling role of education. Later we will develop a model, where education is productive.

Assume that the worker's type is the private information of the worker and is not observed by the market. The worker can however obtain some education. The cost of obtaining e years of education depends on the worker's type and is given by a function $c(e, \theta)$, where

$$c_e > 0, c_{ee} \geq 0, c_\theta < 0, c_{e\theta} < 0. \tag{8.1}$$

The utility of the worker who gets wage w and spends e years in school is

$$u(w, e) = w - c(e, \theta). \tag{8.2}$$

The first two assumptions on the cost function state that it is an increasing convex function, i.e., both cost and MC increase in e. The third assumption states that the cost of education is decreasing in type, which justifies interpreting θ as the ability. The last assumption states that the MC of education decreases with ability, that is, it is not only easier for a more able person to graduate from the university but it is also easier for her to get an extra year of education than for a least able person with the same educational level. This property is known as the *single crossing property*. The name comes from the fact that if on draws the indifference curves for both types in (e, w) space passing through the same point, at the crossing point, the indifference curve for the lower type is steeper than for the higher type, and therefore they can cross only once. This property is crucial for the existence of a separating WPBE, i.e., of a WPBE were different types select different education levels.

The labor market is assumed to be competitive, i.e., firms pay a wage equal to the expected productivity given the education. The WPBEs of the game can be divided into two groups: pooling and separating. In a separating equilibrium, different types obtain different educational levels. A separating WPBE in this game is a strategy $e(\theta)$, a wage schedule $w(e)$ and a belief $\Pr(\theta = \theta_H | e)$ such that,

$$e(\theta) \in \arg\max(w(e) - c(e, \theta)), \tag{8.3}$$
$$w(e) = \Pr(\theta = \theta_H | e)\theta_H + (1 - \Pr(\theta = \theta_H | e))\theta_L, \tag{8.4}$$
$$\Pr(\theta = \theta_H | e(\theta_H)) = 1, \quad \Pr(\theta = \theta_H | e(\theta_L)) = 0. \tag{8.5}$$

Unfortunately, the market has infinitely many WPBEs. Indeed, define e^* and e^{**} by

$$\theta_H - c(e^*, \theta_L) = \theta_L, \tag{8.6}$$
$$\theta_H - c(e^{**}, \theta_H) = \theta_L. \tag{8.7}$$

By the single crossing property, $e^* < e^{**}$. Here, e^* is the education level such that a low type is indifferent between getting wage θ_H and obtaining education level e^* and getting wage θ_L and obtaining no education at all and e^{**} is the education level such that a high type is indifferent between getting wage θ_H and obtaining education level e^{**} and getting wage θ_L

and obtaining no education at all. Then for any $\widetilde{e} \in [e^*, e^{**}]$, the following strategies and beliefs constitute a separating WPBE

$$e(\theta_L) = 0, \tag{8.8}$$

$$e(\theta_H) = \widetilde{e}, \tag{8.9}$$

$$w(e) = \begin{cases} \theta_L, & e < \widetilde{e} \\ \theta_H, & e \geq \widetilde{e}, \end{cases} \tag{8.10}$$

$$\Pr(\theta = \theta_H | e) = \begin{cases} 0, & e < \widetilde{e} \\ 1, & e \geq \widetilde{e}. \end{cases} \tag{8.11}$$

If $\widetilde{e} > e^*$, the equilibrium can be supported by different beliefs as long as probability of θ_H remains sufficiently low for $e < \widetilde{e}$. Note, however, that in any separating WPBE $e(\theta_L) = 0$.

The pooling equilibrium is the equilibrium where both types obtain the same education. Let λ be the fraction of the high types in the population, then,

$$E\theta = \lambda\theta_H + (1 - \lambda)\theta_L. \tag{8.12}$$

Define e' by,

$$E\theta - c(\theta_L, e') = \theta_L, \tag{8.13}$$

and let $\widehat{e} \in [0, e']$. Then the following strategies and beliefs constitute a WPBE,

$$e(\theta_L) = e(\theta_H) = \widehat{e}, \tag{8.14}$$

$$w(e) = E\theta, \tag{8.15}$$

$$\Pr(\theta = \theta_H | e) = \lambda. \tag{8.16}$$

8.2.2 *The intuitive criterion*

Though there are a plethora of WPBEs in the game, only one of them is intuitively sensible. To understand what is meant by, intuitively sensible consider a WPBE and let the high type worker deviate from her strategy and obtain some educational level $e_d \neq e(\theta_H)$ for that particular equilibrium. Suppose that after that she makes the following speech during her job interview with a prospective employer: "Suppose I am a low type worker, then I would have preferred the equilibrium wage and education level that accord to my type to wage θ_H and education e_d. Therefore, I would have had no incentives to deviate and fool you into my being high type. Therefore, I am a high type worker." The credibility of this statement depends upon whether there exists such level e_d for which it is true. It turns out that such e_d exists for all WPBE except for the separating equilibrium with $e(\theta_H) = e^*$. Indeed, for any other $\widetilde{e}$ just take any $e_d \in (e^*, \widetilde{e})$. For any pooling equilibrium define e_1 and e_2 by,

$$\theta_H - c(e_1, \theta_L) = E\theta - c(\widehat{e}, \theta_L), \qquad (8.17)$$
$$\theta_H - c(e_2, \theta_H) = E\theta - c(\widehat{e}, \theta_H). \qquad (8.18)$$

By the single crossing property, $e_1 < e_2$. Select any $e_d \in (e_1, e_2)$. So, the only WPBE for which the speech is not credible is the separating one with $e(\theta_H) = e^*$. The criterion of selection used here is a particular case of the Cho and Kreps' intuitive criterion.

8.3   The competitive screening model

The basic difference between the signaling and the screening model is that now the uninformed party (the employer or the insurance company) moves first and devises a wage schedule (or an insurance premium schedule): $w = w(s)$. The workers then choose s to maximize,

$$u_W(\theta, w(s), s) = w(s) - c(s, \theta).$$

The relevant equilibrium concept here is the Bayesian–Nash equilibrium (BNE) (see the section on the games with incomplete information). Here, an equilibrium, if exists, is unique.

Such sensitivity of the results to the modeling assumption (who makes the first move) is rather disturbing. One can think that this is just a modeling assumption and there is no good way to distinguish the two situations in reality.

8.3.1   *A screening model of education*

As in the basic Spence model, there are two types of workers, $\theta \in \{\theta_L, \theta_H\}$. Assume that the type of the worker is equal to her productivity and is the private information of the worker, i.e., it is not observed by the market. A firm can try to make workers to reveal their type by engaging in a costly activity, e.g., obtaining education (this costly activity can be either productive or not. For simplicity, we assume that it is not). Therefore each firm makes the following announcement:

> *We have two types of positions to fill. The first position requires minimal education e_L and pays w_L. The second position requires minimal education e_H and pays w_H.*

A worker observes the offers of all the firms and decides whether to take employment at all and if yes at which firm and at which position. The cost of obtaining e years of education depends on type and is given by a function $c(e, \theta)$, where $c(0, \theta) = 0$ and,

$$c_e > 0, c_{ee} \geq 0, c_\theta < 0, c_{e\theta} < 0. \tag{8.19}$$

The utility of the worker who gets wage w and spends e years in school is,

$$u(w, e) = w - c(e, \theta), \tag{8.20}$$

and the utility of a firm is its profit.

Therefore, we have a game of incomplete information. Suppose there are I firms. A strategy of a firm i is a menu of contracts $\{(e_L^i, w_L^i), (e_H^i, w_H^i)\}$ and strategy of the worker of type θ is $\{X, j\}$, where $X : \{\theta_L, \theta_H\} \times_i \{(e_L^i, w_L^i), (e_H^i, w_H^i)\} \to \{0, 1, \ldots, I\}$ is the answer to the question: At which firm do you want to be employed? (0 means on neither) and $j \in \{L, H\}$ is the answer to the question: At which position do you want to be employed?

The relevant equilibrium concept here is a subgame-perfect BNE. Can such a game have a pooling BNE? Recall that in a pooling BNE, $E\theta = w_H = w_L = w$ and $e_H = e_L = e$. Suppose this is the case. But now firm i will have a profitable deviation: offer a new contract (e_H, w_H) such that,

$$w_H - c(e_H, \theta_H) > w - c(e, \theta_H) > w_H - c(e_H, \theta_L), \tag{8.21}$$
$$w_H < \theta_H. \tag{8.22}$$

This is always possible because of the single-crossing property. But this contract will attract only high types and firm i will make profits. Therefore, the initial configuration cannot be an equilibrium. *In a screening game, there are no pooling BNEs.* This is the first main difference from the signaling models.

Recall that the signaling game had infinitely many BNEs. Define e^* and e^{**} by,

$$\theta_H - c(e^*, \theta_L) = \theta_L, \tag{8.23}$$

$$\theta_H - c(e^{**}, \theta_H) = \theta_L. \tag{8.24}$$

By the single crossing property, $e^* < e^{**}$. Here, e^* is the education level such that a low type is indifferent between getting wage θ_H and obtaining education level e^* and getting wage θ_L and obtaining no education at all and e^{**} is the education level such that a high type is indifferent between getting wage θ_H and obtaining education level e^{**} and getting wage θ_L and obtaining no education at all. Then for any $\tilde{e} \in [e^*, e^{**}]$, the following strategies and beliefs constitute a separating BNE,

$$e(\theta_L) = 0, \tag{8.25}$$

$$e(\theta_H) = \tilde{e}, \tag{8.26}$$

$$w(e) = \begin{cases} \theta_L, & e < \tilde{e} \\ \theta_H, & e \geq \tilde{e}, \end{cases} \tag{8.27}$$

$$\Pr(\theta = \theta_H | e) = \begin{cases} 0, & e < \tilde{e} \\ 1, & e \geq \tilde{e}. \end{cases} \tag{8.28}$$

If $\tilde{e} > e^*$ the equilibrium can be supported by different beliefs as long as probability of θ_H remains sufficiently low for $e < \tilde{e}$. Note, however, that in any separating BNE, $e(\theta_L) = 0$. Therefore, in a separating equilibrium of the signaling game, the education level of low type was fixed to be zero but multiple levels of education for the high type could be supported as the equilibrium levels. It turns out that in the screening game, only one of them can be supported as a BNE. First, it can be proven that there can be no cross-subsidization in a separating equilibrium, therefore $w_L = \theta_L$ and $w_H = \theta_H$. Now if all firms require $e_L > 0$, then firm i can deviate, require $e_L = 0$ and set $w_L < \theta_L$ but in such a way that $w_L > \theta_L - c(e_L, \theta_L)$, attract all low type workers and make profits. Therefore, $e_L = 0$.

I claim that the only possible candidates for BNEs are $(0, \theta_L)$, (e^*, θ_H) all workers accept a job, select the highest offer if the offers are equal randomize with arbitrary probability, high types select contract (e^*, θ_H) and low types contract $(0, \theta_L)$. I already argued that the contract designed to attract low types should be $(0, \theta_L)$. Therefore, $e_H \geq e^*$. But if $e_H > e^*$, a firm will decrease both w_H and e_H is such a way that it will attract only high type workers and make profits. Therefore, the only candidate for an equilibrium is the one described above. If,

$$w = \theta_H - c(\theta_H, e^*) > E\theta, \tag{8.29}$$

(there are too few high types) it is indeed an equilibrium. Otherwise it can be beaten by,

$$w_L = w_H \in (w, E\theta), \tag{8.30}$$

$$e_L = e_H = 0. \tag{8.31}$$

A firm that offers such a deal will attract all the workers and make positive profits. Therefore, if there are too many high types, a competitive screening model does not have a BNE.

Note that the low type obtains the efficient level of education and does not suffer from imperfect information. The high type obtains the inefficient level of education (is overeducated) and has lower utility than under the perfect information. The high type will be better off if the type were printed on her forehead. This condition will be reversed in a monopolistic screening model.

8.3.2 *The insurance model*

Consider a competitive insurance market that faces two types of customers: high risks and low risks, i.e., $\theta \in \{\theta_L, \theta_H\}$, where θ is the probability of damage. All customers have initial wealth $W > 0$. Suppose a customer pays an insurance premium r and is entitled to a reimbursement x in the case of the accident. Then,

$$W_1 = W - r, \tag{8.32}$$

$$W_2 = W - r - D + x, \tag{8.33}$$

where W_1 and W_2 are the wealth in the case of no accident and an accident respectively. The expected utility of type θ is,

$$U(W_1, W_2) = \theta u(W_1) + (1 - \theta)u(W_2), \tag{8.34}$$

where $u(\cdot)$ is the customer's Bernoulli utility function. In terms of r and x

$$U(r, x; \theta) = \theta u(W - r) + (1 - \theta)u(W - r + x - D) \Rightarrow \tag{8.35}$$

$$U_{\theta r} = u'(W - r - D + x) - u'(W - r). \tag{8.36}$$

Since u is concave,

$$U_{r\theta} > 0 \tag{8.37}$$

for $x < D$. We will see that this is indeed that the relevant values of x are indeed $x < D$, in equilibrium no one will by more coverage than the actual loss.

The Benchmark Case

Let θ be observable. Then in a competitive market, firms will offer contract $r = \theta x$ to type θ (i.e., the insurance premium will be actuarially fair) and the consumer's will be insured fully (recall an example to Chapter 6 we solved in class), i.e., $W_1 = W_2 \Rightarrow$

$$W - \theta x = W - \theta x - D + x \Rightarrow x = D. \tag{8.38}$$

Note that at this point, the consumer's indifference curves are tangent to the firm's isoprofit lines,

$$\theta x - r = \text{const.} \Rightarrow \theta W_2 + (1 - \theta)W_1 = \text{const.} \tag{8.39}$$

Private Information Case

In this case, the firms offer a menu of contracts (r_L, x_L) and (r_H, x_H). Reasoning in exactly the same way as for the model of education we can prove the following series of propositions.

Proposition 1. *No pooling BNE exists.*

Indeed, it is always possible to break any candidate for such an equilibrium by offering a contract that will affect only low risks.

Proposition 2. *In any separating BNE, the high risks (bad types) are fully insured.*

Proposition 3. *If there are enough high risks, then the unique BNE exists with the high risks fully insured and the low risks less then fully insured and being offered the contract that leaves the high risks indifferent between their contract and the low type contract.*

8.4 The monopolistic screening model

Assume a monopolist can produce a unit of good with quality x at a cost $c(x)$, where $c(x)$ is a strictly convex, twice differentiable function. Monopolist is risk neutral. Preferences of a consumer over a unit of good with quality x are given by a twice continuously differentiable utility function $u(\theta, x)$. Preferences of consumers are quasilinear in money:

$$v(\theta, x, m) = u(\theta, x) + m.$$

Each consumer wants to buy at most one unit of the monopolist's goods. Type θ is private information of a consumer. However, it is common knowledge that the type is distributed according to a distribution $f(\theta)$ for each consumer. The distribution has compact support (for concreteness $\theta \in (0, 1)$) and $f(\theta) > 0$. If consumer does not purchase a good from the monopolist, she receives utility $u_0(\theta)$. For simplicity, assume it does not depend on type and normalize it to be zero. Finally, assume

$$u_1 > 0, \ u_2 > 0, \ u_{12} > 0.$$

(Here u_i is the derivative of u with respect to the ith argument, u_{12} is the cross partial derivative with respect to θ and x). The last of this conditions is known as *the Spence–Mirrlees condition or the single-crossing property*. The monopolist and the consumers play the following game:

1. The monopolist specifies the message space M and commits to sell a consumer a good of quality $x(m)$ for price $t(m)$ for every $m \in M$.
2. A consumer decides whether to participate and if yes sends a message $m(\theta)$.
3. Payoffs are realized.

A strategy of a consumer is a function from $(0, 1)$ into M. We may think of it in a following way. At time zero, consumer does not know her type. The uncertainty is to be resolved by Nature at date one. Consumer chooses a fully contingent plan at time zero. A NE in such a game is called BNE.

Proposition 4 (*The Revelation Principle*). *Let $(t(m), x(m); m(\theta))$ be a BNE in a message game. Then there exists another mechanism such that $M = (0, 1)$, $m(\theta) = \theta$ on the equilibrium path and the monopolist gets the same payoffs as in the initial mechanism.*

Intuitively, in equilibrium the monopolist can deduce the type from the message sent, so why not to ask for it directly. The revelation principle tells that without loss of generality, one may restrict attention to the truth telling mechanisms. Another important fact is given by the *taxation principle*.

Proposition 5 (*Taxation Principle*). *Without loss of generality, the monopolist can restrict her choice of a mechanism to a choice of a nonlinear tariff* $t(x)$.

Using the revelation and the taxation principles, the monopolist's problem without loss of generality can be represented by:

$$\max \int_0^1 (t(x) - c(x))f(\theta)d\theta$$
$$\text{s.t. } x(\theta) \in \arg\max(u(\theta, x) - t(x))$$
$$\max(u(\theta, x) - t(x)) \geq 0.$$

8.4.1 *The monopolistic screening: the case of two types*

Let us concentrate on the case $\theta \in \{\theta_L, \theta_H\}$. Then the integral should be replaced by the sum,

$$\max p_H(t_H - c(x_H)) + (1 - p_H)(t_L - c(x_L)),$$

where $p_H = \Pr(\theta = \theta_H)$ and the constraints become

$$u(x_L, \theta_L) - t_L \geq 0, \tag{8.40}$$
$$u(x_L, \theta_L) - t_L \geq u(x_H, \theta_L) - t_H, \tag{8.41}$$
$$u(x_H, \theta_H) - t_H \geq 0, \tag{8.42}$$
$$u(x_H, \theta_H) - t_H \geq u(x_L, \theta_H) - t_L. \tag{8.43}$$

Constraints (8.40) and (8.42) state that both types would like to participate in the contract and are known as the *individual rationality* constraints, and the constraints (8.41) and (8.43), known as the *incentive compatibility* constraints, ensure that no one would like to choose the contract meant for the other type. The basic results is Stole's *constraint reduction theorem* that states that for the optimal allocation only two of these constraints bind: (8.40) and (8.43): that is, the lowest type gets her reservation utility (in this case, zero) and the high type gets the *information rent* that is just enough to prevent her from pretending to be the low type. This implies that:

$$t_L = u(x_L, \theta_L),$$
$$t_H = u(x_H, \theta_H) - u(x_L, \theta_H) + u(x_L, \theta_L).$$

Therefore, the monopolist's solve

$$\max p_H(u(x_H, \theta_H) - u(x_L, \theta_H) + u(x_L, \theta_L) - c(x_H))$$
$$+ (1 - p_H)(u(x_L, \theta_L) - c(x_L)).$$

The first-order conditions are:

$$u_1(x_H, \theta_H) = c'(x_H),$$
$$u_1(x_L, \theta_L) - c'(x_L) = \frac{p_H}{1 - p_H}(u_1(x_L, \theta_H) + u_1(x_L, \theta_L)) > 0.$$

Note that x_H is at the efficient level (no distortions at the top) and x_L below the efficient level. Type θ_H earns the informations rents,

$$I_{21} = u(x_H, \theta_H) - t_H = u(x_L, \theta_H) - t_L = u(x_L, \theta_H) - u(x_L, \theta_L).$$

8.4.2 *The monopolistic screening with two types: Excel implementation*

To see how to implement the monopolistic screening model in Excel, open file Chapter_11.xlsx (Available at: http://www.worldscientific.com/world scibooks/10.1142/10138). There are four choice variable, therefore you need four changing cells. In the file they are cells $B5{:}E5$. The objective is programmed into the cell $F6$. The fundamentals of the model are the following:

$$u(x, \theta) = \theta x, c(x) = cx^2. \tag{8.44}$$

Value of c is in cell $B7$, values of θ_L and θ_H are in cells $B9$ and $D9$ respectively, and the proportion of high types in cell $B6$. The LHSs of the four constraints are programmed into cells $F11{:}F14$ and the RHSs into the cells $G11{:}G14$. Note that this model satisfies the single crossing property, so we know that two constraints bind and two are redundant. In general, however, this need not be the case. The main reason for the single-crossing to fail is multidimensionality of types. For example, assume the firm produces heaters and air-conditions. There are two types of customers: those who have high value for a heather and low for an air-conditioner and those whose preferences are reversed. Single-crossing property is not satisfied in this example and therefore one cannot *a priori* know which constraints will bind. Let us fix $\theta_H = 3$, $c = 1$ and vary two other parameters, θ_L and p_H. One running Solver do not forget to select the solving method to be *GRG Nonlinear* and also demand the changing variable to be non-negative on the top of the other constraints. Observe, that solution always has $x_H = 1.5$. This is the efficient level of production for the high type and reflects the so-called "no distortions at the top" property. Also note that as p_H becomes sufficiently large, x_L becomes zero, i.e., the low type is excluded from the market.

Before we leave this section, a word of warning is due. Suppose you have to solve the problem with

$$u(x, \theta) = \theta\sqrt{x}. \tag{8.45}$$

Since at solution x_L may be zero, numerical iterations can take it into the negative range. Since square root is not defined for negative values, Excel will return an error and give nonsensical results. To avoid such problems, make a change of variables,

$$y = \sqrt{x}, \tag{8.46}$$

before developing the spreadsheet. The same advice applies to any formula that contains expressions that may become undefined in the vicinity of the optimal values.

8.4.3 *The monopolistic screening: the case of continuum of types* *

Assume a monopolist who faces a continuum of consumers produces a good of quality x. The cost of production is assumed to be given by a strictly increasing, convex, twice differentiable function, $c(\cdot)$. Each consumer is interested in consuming at most one unit of the good and has a utility,

$$\alpha x - t, \tag{8.47}$$

where α is her unobservable type distributed on $(0, 1)$ according to a strictly positive, continuous density function $f(\cdot)$, t is the amount of money transferred to the monopolist, and $u(\alpha, x)$ is a continuous function, strictly increasing in both arguments. Consumers have an outside option $u_0(\alpha)$. The monopolist is looking for a mechanism that would maximize her profits.

According to the *Revelation Principle*, one can without loss of generality assume that the monopolist uses direct revelation mechanisms, that is, she announces quantity and price schedules $x(\alpha)$ and $t(\alpha)$ and allows the consumers to announce their type. Moreover, since incentive compatibility implies that the consumers that consume that same bundle should pay the same amount, one can without loss of generality assume that the monopolist simply announces a nonlinear tariff $t(x)$. The last statement, known as the *taxation principle* was first formulated by Rochet (1985).

The above consideration can be summarized by the following model. The monopolist select a continuous function $t : R \to R$ to solve,

$$\max_{t(\cdot)} \int_0^1 (t(x(\alpha)) - c(x(\alpha)))f(\alpha)d\alpha, \qquad (8.48)$$

where $c(x)$ is the cost of producing a good with quality x and $x(\alpha)$ satisfies,

$$x(\alpha) \in \arg\max(u(\alpha, x) - t(x)), \qquad (8.49)$$
$$\max(\alpha x - t(x)) \geq 0. \qquad (8.50)$$

Here I assumed, that the utility of the outside option is type independent and normalized it to be zero.

The first question you have to address is implementability of an allocation. The reason you have to address implementability in the case of continuum of types, but not in the case of a finite type set, is that constraint (8.49) cannot be taken into account in full generality. Instead, we will replace it by a weaker differential constraint, as shown below, which will give rise to a so-called relaxed problem. However, due to the relaxation of the (8.49), we will need to check that the resulting solution is implementable.

Suppose you are given an allocation $x(\alpha)$. Under what conditions does there exist a nonlinear tariff such that (8.49) is satisfied? If such a tariff exists, the allocation is called implementable. Formally, the following definition holds.

Definition 6. An allocation $x(\cdot)$ is called implementable if it is measurable and there exists a measurable function $t(\cdot)$ such that,

$$x(\alpha) \in \arg\max_{x \in R_+} (\alpha x - t(x)). \qquad (8.51)$$

Our first objective is to characterize the set of implementable allocations.

Theorem 7. *Allocation $x(\cdot)$ is implementable if and only if it is increasing.*

Proving necessity is left to you as an exercise. Let us prove the sufficiency.

Proof. Suppose $x(\cdot)$ is increasing. Then it is measurable and we can define the tariff $t(\cdot)$ by

$$t(\beta) = u(\beta, x(\beta)) - \int_0^\beta x(\gamma)d\gamma. \tag{8.52}$$

Note that the pair of functions $x(\cdot)$ and $t(\cdot)$ define a nonlinear tariff $t(x)$ in a parametric form. Consider the decision of a consumer of type α. From her perspective, choosing quality x is equivalent to choosing type β she pretends to be (this statement is a particular case of the Revelation Principle, see Mas-Colell *et al.* (1995) for a discussion), therefore she solves

$$\max_{\beta \in [0,1]} \left((\alpha - \beta)x(\beta) + \int_0^\beta x(\gamma)d\gamma \right). \tag{8.53}$$

Let

$$V(\alpha, \beta) = \left((\alpha - \beta)x(\beta) + \int_0^\beta x(\gamma)d\gamma \right). \tag{8.54}$$

Our objective is to prove that

$$V(\alpha, \alpha) \geq V(\alpha, \beta) \tag{8.55}$$

which implies that

$$\alpha \in \arg\max_{\beta \in [0,1]} \left((\alpha - \beta)x(\beta) + \int_0^\beta x(\gamma)d\gamma \right), \tag{8.56}$$

and therefore tariff (8.52) implements allocation $x(\cdot)$.

To prove (8.55) note that

$$V(\alpha, \alpha) = \int_0^\alpha x(\gamma)d\gamma, \qquad (8.57)$$

and one can transform (8.54) to take the following form:

$$V(\alpha, \beta) = (\alpha - \beta)x(\beta) + \int_0^\beta x(\gamma)d\gamma. \qquad (8.58)$$

Therefore,

$$V(\alpha, \beta) - V(\alpha, \alpha) = \int_\beta^\alpha (x(\beta) - x(\gamma))d\gamma. \qquad (8.59)$$

Suppose that $\alpha \geq \beta$ then $\gamma \geq \beta$ over the integration range, since $x(\cdot)$ is increasing $x(\beta) \leq x(\gamma)$ for all $\gamma \in [\beta, \alpha]$, therefore $V(\alpha, \beta) - V(\alpha, \alpha) \leq 0$. Similar reasoning proves that $V(\alpha, \beta) - V(\alpha, \alpha) \leq 0$ in the case $\alpha \leq \beta$, which completes the proof. □

This theorem allows us to reformulate the monopolist's problem. For this purpose, define consumer's surplus by

$$s(\alpha) = \max_x(\alpha x - t(x)). \qquad (8.60)$$

According to the envelope theorem

$$s'(\alpha) = u_\alpha(\alpha, x). \qquad (8.61)$$

Using the definition of the consumer surplus to exclude the tariff from the monopolist's objective, the problem can be restated as

$$\int_0^1 (\alpha x - s(\alpha) - c(x))f(\alpha)d\alpha \qquad (8.62)$$

s.t. $s'(\alpha) = x$, $s(\alpha) \geq 0$, $x(\cdot)$ is increasing.

One might also ask whether a particular surplus function is implementable. The answer is: A surplus function is implementable if and only if the unique allocation that solves (8.61) is increasing. It is left as an exercise for a reader to show that if a surplus function is implementable, the implementing tariff solves

$$t(x) = \max_\alpha(u(\alpha, x) - s(\alpha)), \qquad (8.63)$$

that is the tariff of a Fenchel conjugate of the surplus.

Let us for a moment ignore the implementability constraint in problem (8.62). The problem we will end up with what is called the relaxed problem. There are three ways to solve it. Before discussing them, however, I will introduce an important economic concept: *the information rent.*

The Concept of the Information Rent

Let us integrate Eq. (8.61) from α_1 to α_2. We will obtain

$$s(\alpha_2) - s(\alpha_1) \equiv I_{12} = \int_{\alpha_1}^{\alpha_2} x(\alpha)d\alpha. \qquad (8.64)$$

Given any incentive compatible allocation $x(\cdot)$, integral (8.64) determines uniquely the information rent type α_2 earns over α_1. Note that the information rent depends only on allocation and does not depend on which incentive compatible mechanism is used to implement it.

The concept of information rent is of central importance to the screening literature and is the key to the understanding of the economic roots of the difference between the unidimensional and the multidimensional case. Intuitively, since in the unidimensional case there exists only one line connecting any two types, the possibility to define the information rents does not put any restrictions on the allocation. This makes the unidimensional model technically simple and amenable to a variety of approaches, which I will discuss in the next section.

In the multidimensional case, however, any two points can be connected by a continuum of paths. Each of them can be used to define the information rent by a formula similar to (8.64). However, for the information rent to be a meaningful economic concept, this integral should be path independent. This puts severe restrictions on the set of implementable allocations and makes the multidimensional problem much harder than the unidimensional one. In particular, this is the main reason why the direct approach, which I describe in the next section, has very limited applicability in the multidimensional case.

Solving the Screening Problem

Consider problem (8.62) and drop for a moment the constraint that $x(\cdot)$ is increasing. The resulting problem is called the relaxed screening problem. Three approaches to the solution of this problem are possible. Let us evaluate

$$-\int_0^1 s(\alpha)f(\alpha)d\alpha = \int_0^1 s(\alpha)d(1 - F(\alpha)) = -s(0) + \int_0^1 s'(\alpha)d(1 - F(\alpha)).$$

Here, $F(\cdot)$ is the cumulative distribution function corresponding to the density function $f(\cdot)$. Using the envelope condition, the monopolist's objective can be rewritten as

$$\int_0^1 (v(\alpha)x - c(x))f(\alpha)d\alpha - s(0), \tag{8.65}$$

where *virtual type*, $v(\alpha)$ is defined by

$$v(\alpha) = \alpha - \frac{1 - F(\alpha)}{f(\alpha)}. \tag{8.66}$$

The profit maximization then implies that $s(0) = 0$ and x is a pointwise maximizer of the integrand. The first-order condition is

$$v(\alpha) = c'(x). \tag{8.67}$$

Assume that virtual type is positive and increasing in type.[1] Then Eq. (8.67) defines an increasing and therefore implementable allocation, which solves the complete problem. Note that for $\alpha = 1$, Eq. (8.67) implies

$$1 = c'(x), \tag{8.68}$$

that is the highest type consumes the good of the efficient quality. This property is known as *no distortion at the top*.

---

[1] If virtual type is increasing but not necessarily everywhere positive, then $x = \max(x^*, 0)$, where x^* solves (8.67).

8.5 Problems

(1) Assume that the cost of obtaining education e for a worker of type θ is,

$$c(e, \theta) = \frac{e^2}{2\theta},$$

and her productivity is $b(e, \theta) = \theta$, where $\theta \in [0, 1]$. The firms are competitive and pay the expected productivity conditional on the observed education, i.e., they offer wage schedule $w(e)$, where $w(e) = E(\theta|e)$. The utility of the worker is given by:

$$u(w, e) = w - c(e, \theta).$$

(a) Assume that the equilibrium is fully separating. Write the first-order condition and the zero profit condition.

(b) Exclude θ from the equation you obtained in (a) and derive a differential equation for the wage schedule.

(c) Solve the differential equation you obtained in (b) subject to the condition $w(0) = 0$ to find the equilibrium wage schedule.

(2) Consider a monopoly producing goods of different quality, x. The cost of production of a good with quality x is,

$$c(x) = \frac{x^2}{2}.$$

The cost is additive across goods. Consumers are interested at buying at most one unit of the good. Preferences of a consumer over these goods can be captured by taste parameter $\theta \in \{\theta_L, \theta_H\}$. The utility of a consumer of type θ who buys a good of quality x and pays t to the monopolist is

$$u(\theta, x, t) = \theta x - t.$$

The probability that $\theta = \theta_L$ is p_L. The monopolist offers a menu of contracts (x_H, t_H) and (x_L, t_L) designed for the high and low types respectively to maximize profits.

(a) Write the constraints contracts (x_H, t_H) and (x_L, t_L) must satisfy.

(b) Which of these constraints bind and why?

(c) Assume $\theta_L = 1$ and $\theta_H = 2$ and find the optimal allocation.

(3) Consider a game in which, first, nature chooses the type of a worker to be $\theta \in \{\theta_1, \ldots, \theta_n\}$ with $\theta_1 < \cdots < \theta_n$ and let $p_i = \Pr(\theta = \theta_i) > 0$.

The earning ability (productivity) of the worker equals her types. The labor market is competitive, so firms pay the workers their expected productivity. After observing her type, the worker can submit herself to a costless test that will reveal her productivity to all firms at the market, therefore a worker's strategy is the decision to submit as function of θ. Show that in any SPNE of the game, all workers with types $\theta > \theta_1$ submit to the test and firms offer wage $w = \theta_1$ to those workers who do not.

(4) Consider a screening model with continuum of types.

(a) Prove that any implementable allocation is increasing.
(b) Assume the types are distributed uniformly on $[a, a + 1]$ for some $a \geq 0$. Compute the virtual type and demonstrate that it is increasing. Find values of a such that all consumers consume positive amount. Repeat for

$$f(\alpha) = \exp(-\alpha), \text{ for } \alpha \geq 0. \tag{8.69}$$

(5) Consider a screening model where a monopolist produces two goods x and y and consumer can be of one of two types $\theta_1 = (1, 3)$ and $\theta_2 = (3, 1)$. Utility of a consumer of type (a, b) are those who buys bundle (x, y) and pay t is given by:

$$ax + by - t. \tag{8.70}$$

The cost of production of bundle (x, y) is,

$$c(x, y) = \frac{c}{2}(x^2 + y^2), \tag{8.71}$$

and fraction of high types is p_H. Formulate the monopolist's problem, develop a spreadsheet and find numerical solution for $c = 1$ and $p_H \in \{0.1, 0.3, 0.5, 0.7, 0.8, 0.9\}$.

References

J. C. Rochet, The taxation principle and multitime Hamilton-Jacobi equations, *Journal of Mathematical Economics* **14**: 113–128, 1985.

A. Mas-Colell, M. D. Whinston, and J. R. Green, *Microeconomic Theory*, Oxford University Press, Oxford, 1995.

Chapter 9

Hidden Action

Here the parties do not have any private information prior to the contracting, but after the contract is signed, one of the parties can take an unobservable action that affects the payoffs of the other party. The leading example in the view of the widespread separation of the ownership and the control is the following: A firm's owners hire a manager to run a firm. The managers chooses the effort level e she is willing to put in her work, $e \in \{e_1, \ldots, e_n\}$ (or $e \in [0, \infty)$). Cost of effort is $C(e)$, where $C(\cdot)$ is an increasing, convex function. Conditional on the effort level e, the firm's profit is distributed according to a cumulative distribution function $F(\pi|e)$ and $e_1 > e_2 \Rightarrow F(\pi|e_1) \leq F(\pi|e_2)$ for all π, i.e., $F(\pi|e_1)$ first-order stochastically dominates $F(\pi|e_2)$ (review the section on the stochastic dominance). This means that effort improves the distribution of profits for the owners (as long as they prefer more to less), but some uncertainty still remains. The manager is risk averse and her Bernoulli utility is given by,

$$u(w, e) = v(w) - C(e).$$

The owners select the wage schedule as the function of the realized profits to solve

$$\max \left(\int (\pi - w(\pi)) dF(\pi|e) \right),$$

subject to

$$e \in \arg\max \left(\int v(w(\pi)) dF(\pi|e) - C(e) \right)$$

$$\max(\smallint v(w(\pi)) dF(\pi|e) - C(e)) \geq \overline{u},$$

where $\bar{u}$ is the reservation wage. Define

$$B(e) = \int \pi dF(\pi|e),$$

and let

$$C_{\text{SB}}(e) = \min \int w(\pi) dF(\pi|e),$$

subject to

$$e \in \arg\max \left(\int v(w(\pi)) dF(\pi|e) - C(e) \right),$$

$$\max(\int v(w(\pi)) dF(\pi|e) - C(e)) \geq \bar{u},$$

i.e., $B(e)$ is the expected benefit from effort e and $C_{\text{SB}}(e)$ is the cost of implementing this effort. Then the owners' problem can be separated into two steps:

We will always assume that the owners are risk-neutral. If the manager is also risk-neutral, then the best contract is:

$$w = \pi - K,$$

where K is the maximal number, which will still make the owner take the contract. This contract simply sells the enterprise to the manager and makes her the residual claimant for the profits. This provides her with the right incentives, but also makes the manager to bear all the risk of the project. The problem of *moral hazard* is to find the optimal trade-off between the risk-sharing and the incentives provision.

Example 1. Let $e \in \{e_L, e_H\}$ and $\pi \in \{\pi_L, \pi_H\}$, where $e_H > e_L$ and $\pi_H > \pi_L$. The cost of effort is $C(e_H) = c_H$ and $C(e_L) = c_L$ and the probabilities of high profit are given by,

$$p_H = \Pr(\pi_H|e_H) > q_H = \Pr(\pi_L|e_L).$$

The manager's utility is,

$$u(w, e) = v(w) - C(e),$$

for some concave increasing $v(\cdot)$. First, suppose that the owner wants to implement the effort level c_L, then she should simply give the manager a constant wage equal to c_L (if she ties the wage to profits, she will have to pay more on average, since the manager is risk averse). Now suppose that the owner wants to implement the effort level e_H. A constant wage will not do the trick, since the manager will always choose the effort level c_L in response to it. Therefore, the owner will propose a pair of wages w_H and w_L depending on the profits realization, which will solve

$$\min(p_H w_H + (1 - p_H)w_L),$$

subject to

$$p_H v(w_H) + (1 - p_H)v(w_L) - c_H \geq \bar{u}$$
$$p_H v(w_H) + (1 - p_H)v(w_L) - c_H \geq q_H v(w_H) + (1 - q_H)v(w_L) - c_L,$$

the first of the constraints ensures that the manager participates in the contract and the second that she does not shirk. Both of the constraints should bind, otherwise at least one of the wages can be reduced, which will decrease the expected cost for the owner. Therefore,

$$w_H = v^{-1}\left(c_H + \bar{u} + \frac{1 - p_H}{p_H - q_H}(c_H - c_L)\right),$$
$$w_L = v^{-1}\left(c_H + \bar{u} - \frac{p_H}{p_H - q_H}(c_H - c_L)\right).$$

The owner will select to implement effort e_H iff:

$$p_H(\pi_H - w_H) + (1 - p_H)(\pi_L - w_L) \geq q_H \pi_H + (1 - q_H)\pi_L - c_L. \quad (9.1)$$

In the next example, I assume that the effort can take continuum of different values.

Example 2. Let the gross profit of the principal be given by

$$\Pi = z + \varepsilon, \quad (9.2)$$

where z is effort undertaken by the agent, and ε is random noise with zero mean and variance σ^2. Only Π is observable by the principal and verifiable by both parties. The utility of the agent is given by:

$$U = E(w) - \frac{\phi}{2}\text{Var}(w) - \frac{z^2}{2}, \quad (9.3)$$

where w is the agent's payment (wage) conditioned on z through Π. This utility can be derived as the certainty equivalent for the agents with CARA Bernoulli utility assuming that ε is distributed normally. The principal wants to maximize expected profits net of the wage, subject to the incentive compatibility constraint

$$z \in \arg\max \left(E(w) - \frac{\phi}{2}\text{Var}(w) - \frac{z^2}{2} \right), \tag{9.4}$$

and the individual rationality (participation) constraint

$$E(w) - \frac{\phi}{2}\text{Var}(w) - \frac{z^2}{2} \geq 0. \tag{9.5}$$

I will concentrate attention on affine payment schemes

$$w = \alpha\Pi + \beta. \tag{9.6}$$

It is straightforward to show that the optimal affine contract has

$$\alpha = \frac{1}{1 + \phi\sigma^2}, \quad \beta = \frac{\phi\sigma^2 - 1}{2(1 + \phi\sigma^2)^2}. \tag{9.7}$$

To see this, note that α is chosen to maximize the total surplus W defined as

$$W = E(U + \Pi - w), \tag{9.8}$$

subject to (9.4), and β is chosen to insure that (9.5) holds. Since in this case the objective function of the agent is strictly concave, the incentive constraint can be replaced by the first-order condition $z = \alpha$. Plugging this into (9.8) and solving the maximization program one obtains (9.7). The net profit of the principal and the utility of the agent under the optimal affine compensation scheme are given by

$$E(\Pi - w) = \frac{1}{2(1 + \phi\sigma^2)}, \quad U = 0. \tag{9.9}$$

One can see that the slope α of the optimal compensation scheme and the profit of the principal are decreasing in σ, while the utility of the agent is determined by the reservation utility, which is normalized at zero here. Hence, noise damps incentives and dissipates social surplus.

9.1 Non-monotonic incentive schemes

In this section, I provide an example of a situation when the optimal incentive scheme is non-monotone in profits. Think of an agricultural worker who has to choose his level of effort in spring. Once everything is sown, the weather can turn out to be good or bad. If the weather is good, the harvest will be high no matter what the worker did, but if it is bad the harvest has more chances to be medium if the worker worked hard than if he shirked, in which case the harvest is more likely to be low. In that case, medium harvest tells us that the worker probably worked hard, while the high harvest in completely uninformative. Therefore, we would like to pay a higher wage for medium harvest than for high one.

Example 3. Let $e \in \{e_L, e_H\}$ and $\pi \in \{\pi_L, \pi_M, \pi_H\}$, where $e_H > e_L$ and $\pi_H > \pi_M > \pi_L$. The cost of effort is $C(e_H) = c_H$ and $C(e_L) = c_L$. The probability distribution of different levels of profit is given by:

$$p(\pi_H|e_H) = p(\pi_H|e_L) = p, \tag{9.10}$$

$$p(\pi_M|e_H) = p(\pi_L|e_L) = \frac{2}{3}(1-p), \tag{9.11}$$

$$p(\pi_L|e_H) = p(\pi_M|e_L) = \frac{1}{3}(1-p), \tag{9.12}$$

i.e., the probability of the high profits does not depend on effort. Exerting effort shifts probability from the low to medium profit realization. The manager's utility is

$$u(w, e) = v(w) - C(e),$$

for some concave increasing $v(\cdot)$. Let us also assume that the principal wants to implement the level of effort e_H. The principal will propose a triple of wages w_H, w_M, and w_L depending on the profits realization, which will solve

$$\min(p(\pi_H|e_H)w_H + p(\pi_M|e_H)w_M + p(\pi_L|e_H)w_L),$$

subject to

$$p(\pi_H|e_H)v(w_H) + p(\pi_M|e_H)v(w_M) + p(\pi_L|e_H)v(w_L) - c_H \geq \overline{u},$$
$$p(\pi_H|e_H)v(w_H) + p(\pi_M|e_H)v(w_M) + p(\pi_L|e_H)v(w_L) - c_H$$
$$\geq p(\pi_H|e_L)v(w_H) + p(\pi_M|e_L)v(w_M) + p(\pi_L|e_L)v(w_L) - c_L.$$

Let λ be the multiplier for the individual rationality constraint and μ is the multiplier for the incentive compatibility constraint. Then the first-order conditions are:

$$\frac{1}{v'(w_i)} = \lambda + \mu\left(1 - \frac{p(\pi_i|e_L)}{p(\pi_i|e_H)}\right), \tag{9.13}$$

where $i \in \{L, M, H\}$. Since $\frac{1}{v'(w_i)}$ is increasing in w_i (recall that $v(\cdot)$ is concave) and $\mu > 0$, (otherwise, the first-order conditions will imply $w = const$ and IC will be violated) the wage is increasing in the likelihood ratio

$$\mathrm{LR}(\pi_i) = \frac{p(\pi_i|e_H)}{p(\pi_i|e_L)}. \tag{9.14}$$

Therefore, wage increases in profits if and only if right hand side of (9.14) is increasing in profits (this property is known as monotone likelihood ratio [MLRP] property). Note that $MLRP \Rightarrow FOSD$ but reverse is not true. For example, with the probability distributions given in this example

$$\mathrm{LR}(\pi_H) = 1, \ \mathrm{LR}(\pi_M) = 2, \ \mathrm{LR}(\pi_L) = \frac{1}{2}, \tag{9.15}$$

therefore $w_M > w_H > w_L$.

Note that the above contract will not be feasible if the agent has an opportunity to destroy the output. In that case, we have to impose the monotonicity constraint exogenously.

9.2 Moral hazard in teams

So far we concentrated on costs of separation of the ownership from the control. Such separation, however, can have its positive side and alleviate the free-riding problems in organizations were collective effort is required. Let us consider the following problem: n agents form a partnership (e.g., a law firm). Each agents decides to exert some level of effort $e_i \in [0, \infty)$. The private cost of effort is given by increasing, differentiable, convex function $c_i(\cdot)$ such that $c_i(0) = c_i'(0) = 0$. The last condition will guarantee that everyone will choose a positive effort. The output is given by:

$$x = \sum_{i=1}^{n} e_i. \tag{9.16}$$

Assume that this output is sold at price one and the proceeds are shared equally among the agents, i.e., amount of money agent i gets is,

$$m_i = \frac{x}{n}. \tag{9.17}$$

The utility of agent i is assumed to be:

$$u(m_i, e_i) = m_i - c_i(e_i). \tag{9.18}$$

Let us find the Nash equilibrium of the game where each agent chooses their effort level independently. For this purpose, fix the effort levels of each individual except for i and consider the problem of agent i. Let,

$$e_{-i} = \sum_{j=1, j \neq i}^{n} e_j. \tag{9.19}$$

Then agent i solves

$$\max \left(\frac{1}{n}(e_{-i} + e_i) - c_i(e_i) \right), \tag{9.20}$$

therefore,

$$c'(e_i^{\mathrm{NE}}) = \frac{1}{n}. \tag{9.21}$$

Let us compare it with the efficient level of effort. It solves

$$\max \left(\sum_{i=1}^{n} (e_i - c_i(e_i)) \right), \tag{9.22}$$

therefore,

$$c'(e_i^{\mathrm{PO}}) = 1. \tag{9.23}$$

Since $c'(\cdot)$ is increasing we see that

$$e_i^{\mathrm{NE}} < e_i^{\mathrm{PO}}. \tag{9.24}$$

Therefore, in equilibrium agents underprovide effort. Can the problem be solved if agents use more sophisticated sharing rules? The answer is "No" provided that they do never throw away the output. Indeed, let $m_i = s_i(x)$, where

$$\sum_{i=1}^{n} s_i(x) = x. \tag{9.25}$$

Then agent i solves

$$\max(s_i(x) - c_i(e_i)), \tag{9.26}$$

and the first-order condition is

$$s_i'(x) = c_i'(e_i). \tag{9.27}$$

Suppose there exists $s_i(\cdot)$ such that $e_i = e_i^{PO}$ for all i, then,

$$s_i'(x) = 1. \tag{9.28}$$

But (9.25) implies that,

$$\sum_{i=1}^{n} s_i'(x) = 1, \tag{9.29}$$

which is a contradiction as long as $n > 1$. Therefore, as long as we insist on (9.25), it is impossible to provide optimal incentives. The problem can be solved if one brings into the organization the budget breaker. In that case, consider a contract

$$s_i(x) = \begin{cases} e_i^{PO} & \text{if } x \geq ne_i^{PO}, \\ 0 & \text{if } x < ne_i^{PO}, \end{cases} \tag{9.30}$$

and assume for simplicity that $c_i(\cdot) = c(\cdot)$. Then for such a contract $e_i = e_i^{PO}$ is a NE. If the output fails below the level specified, the budget breaker gets all the money. Note that budget breaker can be paid some positive amount even in equilibrium, as long as this amount is small enough so the agents still have the incentive to perform.

The same ideas will work even if we introduce in the system some uncertainty. This example shows why a capitalistic firm may be preferable to a partnership and emphasizes some positive sides of separation of the ownership and control.

9.3 Problems

(1) Suppose effort can take three possible values $\{e_1, e_2, e_3\}$ and there are two possible profit outcomes $\pi_H = 10$ and $\pi_L = 0$. The probabilities if the high profit are $p(\pi_H|e_1) = 2/3$, $p(\pi_H|e_2) = 1/2$, $p(\pi_H|e_3) = 1/3$. The agent's cost of effort is $c(e_1) = 5/3$, $c(e_2) = 8/5$, $c(e_3) = 4/3$. The owner is risk-neutral and the manager is risk-averse with Bernoulli utility

$$u(w, e) = \sqrt{w} - c(e).$$

The utility of the outside option, $\bar{u} = 0$.

(2) (1) Prove that the distribution of profits $F(\pi|e_1)$ FOSD $F(\pi|e_2)$ FOSD. $F(\pi|e_3)$.
(2) Find the cost of implementing each level of effort.
(3) Find the optimal contract.

Chapter 10

Introduction to Auctions

Auctions are common institutions to sell goods ranging from houses to pieces of art and spectrum rights. The four standard auctions are: the first-price sealed bid auction, where bidders submit sealed bids, the highest bidder wins and pays her bid; the second-price sealed bid auction where bidders submit sealed bids, the highest bidder wins and pays the second highest bid; an English auction where the seller starts from a low price and increases it until only one bidder is in, the good is sold at that price; and a Dutch auction, where the seller begins with a very high price and decreases it until the first bidder agrees to buy the good.

Consider two auctions scenarios. Scenario one features an auction of an item of modern art, while scenario two features an auction for the oil drilling rights. In the first auction, the value a bidder assigns to a work of art is determined by her personal taste. We will call such values private. In the second case, the value of the right depends on how much oil is there in the ground. It is the same for all bidders. We will call such value common. The value of the object for an auctioneer is determined by signals she gets. Examples of signals are: the bidders private taste for a piece of art, opinions of art experts on the quality of piece of art, estimates of the amount of oil in the ground obtained in survey missions. In general,

$$v_i = v_i(s_1, \ldots, s_N), \tag{10.1}$$

i.e., the value of an object depends on the signals obtained by all individuals.

The signals can be distinguished along different dimensions. First, they can be either dependent or independent. *A priori* (before I or an art expert looks at a piece of art, or before a survey mission is conducted) the signals can be considered as random variables. Therefore, we can call them independent iff the corresponding random variables are independent.

Another dimension along which signal can differ is being unidimensional or multidimensional. In the first case the signal is just a number, for example, my personal taste for a piece of art, the result of one survey mission. In the second case it is a vector. For example, my personal taste for a piece of art and the opinion of an expert results of two survey missions.

10.1 Independent private values model

Since signals are considered to be random variables, they are characterized by a joint distribution function $F(s_1, \ldots, s_N)$. Independence means that

$$F(s_1, \ldots, s_N) = F(s_1) \cdot \ldots \cdot F(s_N). \tag{10.2}$$

Private values means that

$$v_i = v_i(s_i), \tag{10.3}$$

i.e., the individual's value depends only on her own signal. For example, if I buy a piece of art without the intention to resell, the only thing that counts is my private valuation and I assume these valuation to be independent among the bidders. Though that s_i can be a vector, the bidding behavior will depend only on v_i and the belief about the valuations of the other bidders. If the signals are independent so are the valuations, therefore from now on we drop the reference to signals.

10.1.1 *Analysis of the four standard auctions*

Let us now analyze the four standard auctions, we mentioned above. First, note that the first-price sealed bid auction, is strategically equivalent to the Dutch auction. Indeed, a strategy in the first-price sealed bid auction is a bidding function $b_i(s_i)$, while a strategy in the Dutch auction is an entry price function $p_i(s_i)$.

The equivalence is established by

$$b_i(s_i) = p_i(s_i), \tag{10.4}$$

and holds in all environments.

One might guess that the second-price sealed bid auction is strategically equivalent to the English auction: just identify your bid in the second-price sealed bid auction with your exit price in the English auction. However, this is not quite true. Indeed, in the English auction, you can condition your exit price on the decisions of the others, but you cannot do it in a sealed-bid format. In the private values environment, however, such a conditioning is useless. After eliminating those strategies, the two auctions become strategically equivalent.

Equilibria in the Second-price Sealed Bid Auction

First, let us argue that,

$$b_i(v_i) = v_i, \tag{10.5}$$

is a weakly dominating strategy in the second-price sealed bid auction. Indeed, assume that for some valuation bidder i bids below her valuation, i.e., there exists v_i such that,

$$b_i(v_i) < v_i. \tag{10.6}$$

By increasing her bid up to v_i, she will increase the probability to win, while leaving the payment in the case of winning the same. Note also that she wins only if the second highest bid is below v_i, i.e., her realized surplus is always non-negative. Therefore, increasing the bid is weakly increasing her payoff.

Now let us assume that for some valuation bidder i bids above her valuation, i.e., there exists v_i such that,

$$b_i(v_i) > v_i. \tag{10.7}$$

By decreasing her bid up to v_i, she will decrease the probability to win and leave the payment in the case of winning the same. Note, however, that the only cases she lost by this decrease are those when she where required to pay above per valuation, i.e., those when the second highest bid was between v_i and b_i. Therefore, her expected payoff has increased.

The strategy profile

$$b_i(v_i) = v_i, \tag{10.8}$$

is the unique symmetric NE in the second-price sealed bid auction. However, there are other asymmetric equilibria. For example, let $v_i \in [0, 1]$ and $N = 2$. Then,

$$\begin{cases} b_1(v_1) = 0, \\ b_2(v_2) = 1, \end{cases} \tag{10.9}$$

constitutes a BNE.

Symmetric Equilibrium in the Hybrid First-price/All-Pay Auction

Let us consider an auction with us following rules. Bidders submit sealed bids. The object goes to the highest bidder who pays her bid. Everyone else pays fraction $a \in [0,1]$ of their bid. By introducing parameter a, we incorporated as limiting cases two kinds of auctions. Case $a = 0$ corresponds to the first-price auction and is one of the four standard auctions considered above. Case $a = 1$ corresponds to the all-pay auction, which provides a good model of political competition.

Let us make the following assumptions. Bidder's i valuation $v_i \in [0,1]$ and be distributed according to the same probability density function $f(\cdot)$ for all bidders. Let $F(\cdot)$ be the corresponding cumulative distribution function, i.e., $F' = f$. We will be looking for a symmetric equilibrium, i.e., an equilibrium where all the bidders use the same bidding function

$$b_i = b(v_i). \tag{10.10}$$

It can be shown that the bidding function should be differentiable and strictly increasing in the bidder's valuation.

Assume all bidders but one follow strategy $b(\cdot)$. If the remaining bidder (call her, without loss of generality, bidder 1) has valuation v and bids as if her valuation were v' her expected payoff will be:

$$U(v, v') = (v - b(v'))p - a(1 - p),$$

where

$$p = \Pr(v' > \max\{v_2, \ldots, v_N\}). \tag{10.11}$$

Note that

$$(v' > \max\{v_2, \ldots, v_N\}) \Leftrightarrow ((v' > v_2) \text{ and } (v' > v_3), \ldots, \text{ and } (v' > v_N)). \tag{10.12}$$

Since the valuations are independent

$$\Pr((v' > v_2) \text{ and } (v' > v_3), \ldots, \text{ and } (v' > v_N))$$

$$= \prod_{i=1}^{N} \Pr(v_i < v') = F^{N-1}(v'), \tag{10.13}$$

and bidder one will now solve

$$\max_{v'}(v - b(v'))F^{N-1}(v') - ab(v')(1 - F^{N-1}(v')). \tag{10.14}$$

The first-order condition will be

$$(F^{N-1}(v') + a(1 - F^{N-1}(v')))b'(v')$$
$$= (N-1)F^{N-2}(v')f(v')(v - (1-a)b(v')). \qquad (10.15)$$

If $b(\cdot)$ is the equilibrium bidding function, it should hold at $v' = v$. Therefore, we get a differential equation on $b(\cdot)$

$$(F^{N-1}(v) + a(1 - F^{N-1}(v)))b'(v) = (N-1)F^{N-2}(v)f(v)(v - (1-a)b(v)). \qquad (10.16)$$

It should be solved subject to the constraint $b(0) = 0$.

Example 1. Let v be distributed uniformly on $[0,1]$, i.e.,

$$f(v) = 1, \quad F(v) = v \qquad (10.17)$$

and let $a = 0$, so we are considering the first-price sealed-bid auction. Then $b(\cdot)$ solves

$$b'(v) = \frac{(N-1)(v - b(v))}{v}, b(0) = 0. \qquad (10.18)$$

Let us look for a solution in a form

$$b(v) = \alpha v. \qquad (10.19)$$

Then α solves

$$\alpha = (N-1)(1-\alpha) \Rightarrow \alpha = \frac{N-1}{N}. \qquad (10.20)$$

Equilibrium bidding strategy is given by

$$b(v_i) = \frac{(N-1)v_i}{N}. \qquad (10.21)$$

Note that while in the second-price sealed-bid auction bidders bid their true values, in the first-price auctions bidders shade their bids. To get the intuition, note that in lowering the bid by dv, the bidder trades off two effects: an increase in the expected payoff if she wins the auction versus a decrease in the probability of winning. The marginal benefit (MB) due to the first effect is given by

$$MB = b'(v)F^{N-1}(v)dv, \qquad (10.22)$$

while the marginal cost (MC) incurred due to the second effect is

$$MC = (v - b)[F^{N-1}(v)]'dv. \qquad (10.23)$$

The differential equation (10.18) can be written as

$$MB = MC. \qquad (10.24)$$

10.1.2 *A general incentive compatible mechanism*

Note that in the case of symmetric valuations, all standard auctions will allocate the object to the bidder who values its most, i.e., they will all be efficient.[1] Let us ask what can be said about the revenues to the seller. To answer this question, let us consider any incentive compatible mechanism of allocating the object. By the revelation principle, we may assume without loss of generality that the seller commits to the rules that specify probabilities that the good will be allocated to a particular bidder and payments made by the bidders as function of their announced types. The above mentioned probabilities and the payments should satisfy: *incentive compatibility constraints* (everyone should find it in her best interest to tell the truth) and *individual rationality constraints* (everyone would like to participate). Faced with probabilities

$$p_i(v'_1, \ldots, v'_n) \qquad (10.25)$$

and payment

$$t_i(v'_1, \ldots, v'_n), \qquad (10.26)$$

define

$$u_i(v_i, v'_i) = v_i E p_i(v'_1, \ldots, v'_n) - E t_i(v'_1, \ldots, v'_n)$$
$$s_i(v_i) = \max u(v_i, v'_i) = u(v_i, v_i) \qquad (10.27)$$

---

[1]If model is asymmetric, i.e., the valuation of the bidders come from different distributions, then the second-price sealed-bid auction remains efficient, while other formats may in general result in an inefficient allocation.

$u_i(v_i, v_i')$ is the expected utility of type v_i who pretends to be type v_i'. The surplus, $s(v_i)$, of type v_i is her expected utility maximized over the announced type. Since the mechanism is IC, the maximum is achieved at $v_i' = v_i$. By the envelope theorem for the unconstraint optimization

$$\frac{\partial s_i(v_i)}{\partial v_i} = Ep_i(v_1, \ldots, v_n) \equiv q_i(v_i). \tag{10.28}$$

Here $q_i(\cdot)$ is the expected probability that individual i will win the object. You will be asked in a problem in this chapter to show that incentive compatibility requires that $q_i(\cdot)$ is increasing. Integrating

$$s_i(v_i) = s_i(0) + \int_0^{v_i} q_i(t)dt, \tag{10.29}$$

and

$$Et_i(v_1, \ldots, v_n) \equiv c_i(v_i) = v_i q_i(v) - \int_0^{v_i} q_i(t)dt - s_i(0). \tag{10.30}$$

The Seller's Revenue

The sellers expected revenue is given by

$$R = \sum_{i=1}^{N} Ec_i(v_i). \tag{10.31}$$

To evaluate it, let us write

$$Ec_i(v_i) = \int_0^1 c_i(v_i)f(v_i)dv_i, \tag{10.32}$$

and recall that

$$c_i(v_i) = v_i q_i(v) - \int_0^{v_i} q_i(t)dt - s_i(0). \tag{10.33}$$

Let us consider the term

$$-\int_0^1 \left(\int_0^{v_i} q_i(t)dt \right) f(v_i)dv_i = \int_0^1 \left(\int_0^{v_i} q_i(t)dt \right) d(1 - F(v_i)). \tag{10.34}$$

Performing integration by parts,[2]

$$\int_0^{v_i} q_i(t)dt(1-F(v_i))|_0^1 - \int_0^1 (1-F(v_i))q_i(v_i)dv_i = -\int_0^1 (1-F(v_i))q_i(v_i)dv_i.$$

(10.35)

Therefore, the seller's revenue can be written as

$$R = \sum_{i=1}^n \left(\int_0^1 \theta(v_i)f(v_i)q_i(v_i)dv_i - s_i(0) \right),$$

(10.36)

where the virtual type $\theta(v_i)$ is defined by

$$\theta(v_i) = v_i - \frac{1 - F(v_i)}{f(v_i)}.$$

(10.37)

Note that formula (10.36) implies that any two mechanisms that have identical expected probabilities of winning and leave the same surplus to the lowest type generate the same expected revenue to the seller. This fact is known as the *Revenue Equivalence Theorem*. In particular, we call a mechanism *efficient* if it always allocated the good to the individual that values it most. Under the assumption of symmetric valuation, the four standard auctions are efficient, and so is the all-pay auction. Any efficient mechanism that leaves the same surplus to the lowest type generates the same expected revenue to the seller. All four standard auctions generate the same revenue to the seller.

A mechanism is called *optimal* if it maximizes the seller's revenue. According to the individual rationality constraint, $s_i(0) \geq 0$. Therefore, for an optimal mechanism $s_i(0) = 0$. The revenue formula (10.36) implies that in the optimal mechanism, the good should be allocated to the individual with the *highest virtual type* provided it is positive. It should be retained by the seller if the *highest virtual type* is negative. The last statement implies that the optimal mechanism will typically include a reserve price, which is above the seller's valuation. The optimal reserve price, r, is determined from the condition

$$\theta(r) = 0,$$

(10.38)

and is independent from the details of the mechanism and the number of the bidders.

---

[2]See Mathematical Appendix for a discussion of this technique.

The above discussion suggests that even if symmetric independent private value case with risk-neutral bidders, there can be a tension between optimality and efficiency. First, a bidder with the highest virtual type need not be the bidder who values good the most. In that case, the good should be allocated to different bidders under the efficient and the optimal mechanism.

Example 2. For example, let v be distributed on $[\sqrt{2}, +\infty)$ according to density

$$f(v) = \frac{v}{(v^2 - 1)^{3/2}}. \tag{10.39}$$

Then,

$$F(v) = 1 - \frac{1}{\sqrt{v^2 - 1}}, \tag{10.40}$$

and

$$\theta(v) = \frac{1}{v}. \tag{10.41}$$

In an optimal mechanism, the seller would have liked to allocate the good to the lowest type with probability one. However, since incentive compatibility requires that $q_i(\cdot)$ is increasing, the optimal incentive compatible rule in this case is to allocate the good by a fair lottery.

Fortunately, the distribution in the above example is not typical and for the most common distributions this tension does not arise, since the virtual type is increasing in type. Another source of tension comes from optimal auctions having positive reservation price. Four standard auctions without a reserve price are efficient, but not optimal.[3] On the other hand, these auctions with the optimally chosen reserve price will be all optimal, but no longer efficient.

---

[3] They are still optimal in a restricted class of mechanisms that require the reserve price to be equal to the seller's value.

Example 3. Let v_i be distributed uniformly on $[0, 1]$ and let the seller's valuation be zero. Then,

$$\theta(v_i) = 2v_i - 1. \tag{10.42}$$

Therefore, the optimal reserve price is

$$r = 1/2. \tag{10.43}$$

If highest buyer's valuation is less than $1/2$ (say 0.4), the seller should retain the object, which is inefficient.

10.2 Problems

(1) Find an equilibrium of all-pay auction with N bidders and uniform distribution of types (Hint: substitute $a = 1$ and $F(v) = v$ into equation)

$$(F^{N-1}(v) + a(1 - F^{N-1}(v)))b'(v) = (N - 1)F^{N-2}(v)f(v)(v - (1 - a)b(v))$$
$$(10.44)$$

and solve it subject to $b(0) = 0$).

(2) Prove that probability $q_i(t_i)$ of obtaining an object, defined by Eq. (10.28) is weakly increasing in t_i.

Bibliographic notes

Most of the material in this part found its way in the textbooks and as usual Mas-Colell *et al.* (1995) is the best source of advanced treatment. The exceptions are the subsection on the screening with continuum of types and the chapter on Auction theory. The former is based on the original paper by Mussa and Rosen (1978), while the best review of the auction theory is Krishna. Recently, attention has shifted to the so-called multidimensional screening models, where one needs more than one number to specify tastes of the consumers. These literature are very technical, but some important economic results seem to emerge. For example, it is typical in such models that a non-negligible fraction of consumers in not served by the market. For an introduction to mathematics and economics of multidimensional screening, see Basov (2005).

References

S. Basov, *Multidimensional Screening*, Springer-Verlag, Berlin, Germany, 2005.

V. Krishna, *Auction Theory,* Academic Press, Cambridge, MA, USA, 2002.

A. Mas-Colell, M. D. Whinston and J. R. Green, *Microeconomic theory*, Oxford University Press, Oxford, UK, 1995.

M. Mussa, and S. Rosen, Monopoly and product quality, *J. Econ. Theory*, **18**: 301–317, 1978.

PART V

Mathematical Appendix

Overview

In this part, I am going to present the main mathematical tools that we will use during the course. This material is covered during the first week of the mathematical intensive. It is also advisable to return to it from time to time during the course. The formal logic is the set theory where there two pillars at which the modern mathematics stands. In the first chapter, will introduce you to the basics of these fields. In the next two chapters, I will introduce the main ideas of calculus and techniques for solving systems of simultaneous equations. These notes present a more detailed exposition of the topics than you really need to understand to study economics.

The following notation is useful and will be used throughout the course:

$\forall$ — for any,

$\exists$ — there exists,

$\{.\text{list of elements}..\}$ — a set consisting of elements,

$\{x : ..P\}$ — set of all $x's$ such that P holds,

$i = \overline{1, n}$ — i changes from 1 to n,

$\emptyset$ — empty set,

iff $=$ if and only if,

$P \Rightarrow Q$ — P implies Q,

$P \Leftrightarrow Q$ — P logically equivalent to Q,

$h : X \to Y$ reads h is a correspondence (function) from X into Y,

$|z|$ — absolute value of number z,

$A\&B$ or $A \wedge B$ — A and B,

$A \vee B$ — A or B.

Chapter 11

The Formal Logic

Often we need to be able to derive conclusions from the facts we already know. The process of making such conclusions is governed by the rules of formal logic. The formal logic does not allow us to arrive at *new* knowledge, i.e., we cannot learn the laws of physics from the logic alone. It only allows us to draw all the conclusions from what we already know.

11.1 Basics

The main objective of formal logic is to ascertain the truthfulness of complex statements based on the truthfulness of their parts. One starts from a set of simple statements. For example, "$5 \times 5 = 25$," or "Canberra is the capital of Australia." We assume that we know whether such statements are true or false (it is not the job of a logician to discover empirical truths) and use rules of reasoning in to discover whether the complex statements are true. The complex statements are constructible from simple ones using three operations,

(a) Implication: $A \Rightarrow B$.

(b) Conjunction: $A\&B$.

(c) Disjunction: $A \vee B$.

(1) The implication is false if and only if the assumption, A is true and the conclusion, B is false, and is true otherwise. Intuitively, reasoning is unsound if starting from a true premise you arrive at a false conclusion. It is sound if it is not unsound. In particular, a statement "If $3 \times 3 = 10$ then Germany won World War II" is true. It is important to stress that $A \Rightarrow B$ does not mean that A is the *cause* of B. For example, the statement *if*

every differentiable function is continuous then the Earth is approximately 150,000,000 *kilometers from the Sun* is true, though the distance between the Earth and the Sun is determined by the initial conditions and the moment of formation of the Solar System and the force of gravity, rather then by a theorem from a first year calculus.

(2) The statement $A\&B$ is true if and only if both A and B are true.

(3) The statement $A \vee B$ is true if either A or B is true.

11.2 Quantifiers

We sometimes wish to make statements like "for every x statement $P(x)$ is true" or "there exists x such that $Q(x)$ is true." In these statements, "for every x (written as for $\forall x$)" and "there exists x (written as $\exists x$)" are quantifiers. $\forall$ is called a *universal* quantifier, the signed is the letter A up-side-down, where A stands for Any, $\exists$ is called the existential quantifier. A variable under the sign of quantifier is called a *dummy* variable, which means that its name can be changed without affecting the statement. For example, (for $\forall x\ P(x)$) means the same as (for $\forall y\ P(y)$).

11.3 Negated statements

It is important to be able to build negations of the common statements:

(1) $not(A\&B) \Leftrightarrow (not A \vee not B)$,

(2) $not(A \vee B) \Leftrightarrow (not A \& not B)$,

(3) $not(A \Rightarrow B) \Leftrightarrow (A \& not B)$,

(4) $not(A(x)$ for $\forall x \in Y) \Leftrightarrow (\exists x \in Y : not A(x))$,

(5) $not(\exists x \in Y : A(x)) \Leftrightarrow (not A(x)$ for $\forall x \in Y)$.

These rules are quite intuitive. However, they can be used to build negations of any statement, no matter how complicated, which can be hard to do using only intuition.

11.4 Problems

(1) Going through the cases, when an implication is true derive the *modus ponens* rule, i.e., prove that

$$(A\&(A \Rightarrow B)) \Rightarrow B, \tag{11.1}$$

or, in words if A is true and *if A then B* is true then B is true, where A and B stand for any statements.

(2) Prove that if the statement $A \Rightarrow B$ is true, then so too is the statement $\text{not}B \Rightarrow \text{not}A$.

(3) Let A, B, and C be some propositions and assume that the following is true

if A is false and B is true then C is false.

Which of the following statements follow from this theorem?

(a) If A is false then C is true.

(b) If A is true and B is false then C is true.

(c) If either A is false or B is true then C is false.

(d) If C is false then A is false and B is true.

(e) If C is true then both A is false and B is true.

(4) A real number a is called the limit of the sequence of real numbers $\{x_n\}_{n=0}^{\infty}$ if

$$\text{For } \forall \varepsilon > 0 \; \exists n_0 \in N : \text{ for } \forall n > n_0 \; |x_n - a| < \varepsilon. \tag{11.2}$$

Write symbolically the statement "Real number a is not the limit of the sequence of real numbers $\{x_n\}_{n=0}^{\infty}$".

Chapter 12

Basics of Set Theory

The simplest concept which we do not define in the course is that of a set. Intuitively, a set is a collection of any kind. For example, all positive integers, all human beings on Earth. A basic relation is " $\in$ " : $x \in A$ reads "element x belongs to set A."

A warning is important here. Naive usage of the term set can lead to paradoxes. An example is the Russell's paradox.

Example 1. Let X be set of all sets with a property that the set does not contain itself as an element (e.g., set of all human beings on Earth. It contains as its elements all human beings, but not sets of human beings). Question, is $X \in X$ true? Suppose, it is. Then, since X contains only the sets that are not elements of themselves, $X \notin X$. On the other hand, if $X \notin X$, then from the definition of X one would have to conclude that $X \in X$.

Of course, one way out of this paradox is to conclude that a collection of all sets is not a set. But this implies that one needs a formal definition of set. Such a definition was provided by the axiomatic set theory. We will not concern ourselves here with the details. One can always avoid such paradoxes by limiting the universe of discourse (e.g., consider a set of all consumption bundles and functions from the set of such bundles into real numbers).

12.1 Basic operations with sets

Here I introduce basic operations with sets.

153

(a) $A \subset B$ (reads A is a subset of B) iff for $\forall x \in A$ it is true that $x \in B$ (in words, any element of set A is an element of set B).

(b) $x \in A \cap B$ iff $x \in A$ *and* $x \in B$ (the set $A \cap B$ is called the intersection of sets A and B. In words, the intersection of two sets consists of elements that belong to the both sets).

(c) $x \in A \cup B$ iff $x \in A$ *or* $x \in B$ (the set $A \cup B$ is called the union of sets A and B. In words, the union of two sets consists of elements that belong to at least one of the sets).

(d) $x \in A \backslash B$ iff $x \in A$ *and* $x \notin B$ (the set $A \backslash B$ is called the difference of sets A and B.) If $B \subset A$, then $A \backslash B$ is called a complement of B relative to A. If A is a fixed set (universe of discourse), then we will call it simply complement of B and denote B^c.

Definition 2. $A = B$ iff $A \subset B$ and $B \subset A$.

Definition 3. If $\forall x \ x \notin A$, then A is called an empty set ($A = \emptyset$).

Sets A and B are said to be disjoint if $A \cap B = \emptyset$.

$A \times B = \{(x, y) : x \in A \text{ and } y \in B\}$ — Cartesian product of sets A and B.

Let $K \subset X \times Y$ and $(x, y) \in X \times Y$. We will say that $y \in f_K(x)$ iff $(x, y) \in K$. We will call f_K — a *correspondence* from X to Y. Set K is called the graph of correspondence f_K. In words, a correspondence is rule that associates with each point $x \in X$ a subset (possibly empty) of Y. We will typically omit lower indices and refer to correspondences as $f, g, \ldots$.

If for any $x \in X$

$$y_1 \in f(x), \ y_2 \in f(x) \text{ implies } y_1 = y_2,$$

then correspondence f is called a function. In words, a functions associates with any element of X at most one element of Y.

Terminological note:

correspondence = set valued function = multivalued function,

function = map = transformation = operator.

$\text{Im} f = \{y \in Y : \exists x \in X \ y \in f(x)\}$-image or range of correspondence f.

Let $B \subset Y$. Define $f^{-1}(B) = \{x \in X : f(x) \in B\}$-inverse image of set B under correspondence f.

Commonly used notation for some particular sets:

N — natural numbers $\{0, 1, 2, \ldots\}$,

Q — rational numbers $Q = \{x : \exists m \in N \text{ and } n \in N\backslash\{0\} \text{ such that } x = \frac{m}{n} \text{ or } x = -\frac{m}{n}\}$,

R — real numbers.

12.2 Convex sets

An important class of sets, which often arise in economic applications in the class of convex sets. Convex sets arise in the study of preferences, production technologies, or Nash equilibria. A set is called convex if with every two points, it contains the entire line segment connecting those points. More formally,

Definition 4. Set $X \subset R^n$ is called convex if for any $x_1, x_2 \in X$ and any $\lambda \in [0, 1]$,

$$\lambda x_1 + (1 - \lambda)x_2 \in X. \qquad (12.1)$$

Convexity can be defined for sets more general than subsets of R^n, but one needs enough structure to be able to define linear combinations of the elements. In the abstract convexity theory, that finds increasing applications in economics, even this requirement can be lifted. However, this discussion is far beyond the scope of this book.

12.3 Problems

(1) Prove that two sets are equal if and only if they contain the same elements.

(2) Prove that $A \cap (B \cup C) = (A \cap B) \cup (A \cap C)$, $A \cup (B \cap C) = (A \cup B) \cap (A \cup C)$.

(3) Prove that if A and B are convex, then $A \cap B$ is convex. Give an example of two convex sets such that their union is not convex.

Chapter 13

Solutions of Some Equations Systems of Simultaneous Equations

In this chapter, I will introduce you to some methods used to solve the systems of simultaneous equation. Such equations arise in economics, for example, when we look for a system of equilibrium prices or equilibrium strategies in a game (e.g., outputs of Cournot oligopolists), simultaneous movements of the gross domestic product (GDP) and interest rates in macroeconomic models, etc. Let us for simplicity consider here a system of two equations in two variables x and y:

$$\begin{cases} f(x,y) = a, \\ g(x,y) = b. \end{cases} \tag{13.1}$$

One way to solve the system is the consecutive exclusion of variables. The idea of this method is to eliminate one of the variables, say y, from the second equation, i.e., to solve it for y considering x as a parameter. As a result, one will arrive at the following relation:

$$y = \phi(x).$$

Then the first equation becomes

$$f(x, \phi(x)) = a.$$

The strength of this method is that it does not rely on any particular properties of functions f and g, however, in practice, the process of elimination might be impossible to carry out, if the functional forms for f and g are rather complex and even when it is possible, it can be rather cumbersome. However, if the functions f and g are linear, another approach is possible.

13.1 Solving linear equations

A general linear equation is an equation of a form

$$ax + b = c, \qquad (13.2)$$

where $a \neq 0$. To obtain a general solution, take a to the RHS of the equation and divide by a, i.e.,

$$ax = c - b, \qquad (13.3)$$

$$x = \frac{c - b}{a}. \qquad (13.4)$$

Example. $2x + 1 = 3$, $2x = 3 - 1 = 2$, $x = 2/2 = 1$.

Comment. Without loss of generality, one can always assume $c = 0$, since if it is not one can always take it to the LHS of Eq. (13.2) and change the sign. For example, $2x + 1 = 3$ can be re-written as $2x + 1 - 3 = 0$ or $2x - 2 = 0$.

13.2 Quadratic equations

Consider an equation

$$ax^2 + bx + c = 0. \qquad (13.5)$$

The RHS can be assumed to be zero without loss of generality (see the comment in the previous section). If $a = 0$, then the equation is linear and was considered in the previous section. Otherwise, $a \neq 0$ and we can divide both sides of (13.5) by a to obtain

$$x^2 + \frac{b}{a}x + \frac{c}{a} = 0. \qquad (13.6)$$

Transform (13.6) as follows:

$$x^2 + \frac{b}{a}x + \frac{c}{a} = x^2 + 2\frac{b}{2a}x + \frac{b^2}{4a^2} - \frac{b^2}{4a^2} + \frac{c}{a} = 0. \qquad (13.7)$$

Note that

$$\frac{b^2}{4a^2} = \left(\frac{b}{2a}\right)^2, \qquad (13.8)$$

therefore,

$$x^2 + 2\frac{b}{2a}x + \frac{b^2}{4a^2} = \left(x + \frac{b}{2a}\right)^2,$$
(13.9)

and Eq. (13.6) can be re-written as

$$\left(x + \frac{b}{2a}\right)^2 = \frac{b^2}{4a^2} - \frac{c}{a} = \frac{b^2 - 4ac}{4a^2}.$$
(13.10)

Let us introduce a notation

$$D = b^2 - 4ac.$$
(13.11)

One can distinguish three cases:

(1) $D < 0$, in this case the LHS of Eq. (13.10) is non-negative for all real x, since it is a square of some real number, while the RHS is negative, so Eq. (13.10), and therefore an equivalent Eq. (13.5) has no real solutions. It has two complex solutions.[1]

(2) $D = 0$, in which case Eq. (13.10), and therefore an equivalent Eq. (13.5) has one solution:

$$x = -\frac{b}{2a}.$$
(13.12)

Sometimes, it is convenient to talk about two equal solutions.

(3) $D > 0$, in this case Eq. (13.10), and therefore an equivalent Eq. (13.5) has two distinct real solutions:

$$x_{1,2} = \frac{-b \pm \sqrt{D}}{2a}.$$
(13.13)

Example. Consider following equations

$$x^2 + x + 1 = 0,$$
(13.14)

$$x^2 + 3x + 2 = 0,$$
(13.15)

$$x^2 - 2x + 1 = 0.$$
(13.16)

In the first case $D = 1 - 4 = -3 < 0$, so the first equation has no real solutions. In the second case $D = 3^2 - 4*2 = 1$, so the second equation has

---

[1] We do not discuss complex numbers in this course.

two real solutions

$$x_{1,2} = \frac{-3 \pm 1}{2}, \tag{13.17}$$

$$x_1 = -2, \ x_2 = -1. \tag{13.18}$$

In the third case, $D = 2^2 - 4 = 0$, so the only solution is $x = 2/2 = 1$.
Using formula (13.13) one can find:

$$x_1 + x_2 = \frac{-b + \sqrt{D}}{2a} + \frac{-b - \sqrt{D}}{2a} = -\frac{b}{a}. \tag{13.19}$$

$$x_1 * x_2 = \frac{-b + \sqrt{D}}{2a} * \frac{-b - \sqrt{D}}{2a} = \frac{b^2 - (b^2 - 4ac)}{4a^2} = \frac{c}{a}. \tag{13.20}$$

Therefore, one can find the sum and the product of the roots without solving
the equation (in the case of one root one has to treat it as two different,
but equal roots). The statement is known as the *Viet's Theorem*.

Theorem 1 (Viet's Theorem). *Let x_1 and x_2 be the roots a quadratic
equation*

$$ax^2 + bx + c = 0. \tag{13.21}$$

Then,

$$x_1 + x_2 = -\frac{b}{a}, x_1 * x_2 = \frac{c}{a}. \tag{13.22}$$

Remark 2. The theorem is true even if $D < 0$ and the roots are complex.

It is a great way to check whether the solution you found is correct.
For the first equation in the example, $x_1 + x_2 = -2 + (-1) = -3$, and
$x_1 * x_2 = (-2) * (-1) = 2$. For the second equation, $x_1 = x_2 = 1$, and
$x_1 + x_2 = 2$, $x_1 * x_2 = 1$. For the third case, the theorem will still hold for
the complex roots, but we do not consider them in this class.
Using the Viet's theorem, it is easy to prove that

$$ax^2 + bx + c = a(x - x_1)(x - x_2), \tag{13.23}$$

where x_1 and x_2 are the roots of equation,

$$ax^2 + bx + c = 0. \tag{13.24}$$

Indeed, opening the brackets on the RHS of Eq. (13.23), one obtains

$$a(x - x_1)(x - x_2) = ax^2 - a(x_1 + x_2)x + ax_1 * x_2. \tag{13.25}$$

But formula (13.22) implies,

$$-a(x_1 + x_2) = b, \, ax_1 * x_2 = c, \tag{13.26}$$

therefore,

$$a(x - x_1)(x - x_2) = ax^2 + bx + c. \tag{13.27}$$

13.3 Basics of matrix algebra and Cramer's rule

In this section, I am going to develop the basics of matrix algebra.

13.3.1 *Matrices*

The method of solution of system (13.1) developed here is based on matrix algebra. Unlike the method of consecutive exclusion, it works only for linear systems.

A matrix is a rectangular array of numbers

$$A = \begin{matrix} 1 & 0.3 & 4 & 6.1 \\ 0.2 & 2 & 1000 & 4 \\ 0.5 & 11 & 12 & 0 \end{matrix} \quad B = \begin{matrix} 3 & 3 \\ 0 & 2 \end{matrix}$$

If a matrix has n rows and k columns, it is said to have dimension $n \times k$. If $n = k$, a matrix is said to be a square matrix. Let a_{ij} denote the element of matrix A on the intersection of ith row and jth column.

Let A and B be the matrices of the same dimension (say, $n \times k$). Define $C = A + B$ by:

$$c_{ij} = a_{ij} + b_{ij}.$$

Let A is an $n \times k$ matrix, while B is a $k \times m$ matrix. Then define the product $C = A * B$ by

$$c_{ij} = \sum_{\ell=1}^{k} a_{i\ell} b_{\ell j}.$$

Theorem 3. *Let A be an $n \times k$, B be a $k \times m$, and C be an $m \times p$ matrices. Then,*

$$A * (B * C) = (A * B) * C.$$

Proof. Let $P = A*(B*C)$ and $Q = (A*B)*C$, $D = B*C$, and $E = A*B$
Then,

$$p_{ij} = \sum_{x=1}^{n} a_{ix}d_{kx} = \sum_{k=1}^{n} a_{ix}\left(\sum_{y=1}^{n} b_{xy}c_{yj}\right) = \sum_{y=1}^{n}\left(\sum_{k=1}^{n} a_{ix}b_{xy}\right)c_{yj}$$

$$= \sum_{y=1}^{n} e_{iy}c_{yj} = q_{ij}.$$

$\square$

13.3.2 *Determinants and Cramer's rule*

If A is a 1×1 matrix, then define $\det(A) = a_{11}$. If

$$A = \begin{matrix} a_{11} & a_{12} \\ a_{21} & a_{22}, \end{matrix} \tag{13.28}$$

define,

$$\det(A) = a_{11}a_{22} - a_{12}a_{21}. \tag{13.29}$$

Let A be an $n \times n$ matrix. Define,

$$\det A = \sum_{i=1}^{n}(-1)^{1+i}a_{1i}d\det A_{1i}, \tag{13.30}$$

where matrix A_{1i} is obtained from matrix A crossing out the first raw and ith column. Hence, calculation of a determinant of a matrix of size $n \times n$ can be reduced to calculation of determinants of matrices of dimension $(n-1) \times (n-1)$ and so forth, and be eventually reduced to the calculation of a determinant of 1×1 matrix. It is easy to verify that for a 2×2, the determinant is calculated from (13.30) coincides with (13.29).

Cramer's rule (discovered by Gabriel Cramer, 1704–1752) uses the concept of the determinant to arrive at the solution of the system (13.1). First, let us write it in a matrix form,

$$A\mathbf{x} = \mathbf{u},$$

By Cramer's rule, the solutions are given by:

$$x_i = \frac{\det A_i}{\det A},$$

where A_i is derived by substituting vector $\mathbf{u}$ for the ith column of matrix A. Note that if $\det A = 0$ the Cramer's rule does not provide us with a solution. In that case, two things can happen:

(a) A system does not have a solution. For example,

$$\begin{cases} x + y = 1, \\ 2x + 2y = 3. \end{cases}$$

(b) A system has infinitely many solutions

$$\begin{cases} x + y = 1, \\ 2x + 2y = 2. \end{cases}$$

To conclude: a linear system of equation has either one solution, or none, or infinitely many (it *cannot* have exactly 10 solutions, for example).

13.4 Economic applications of systems of simultaneous equations

One of the applications of the systems of simultaneous equations is solving for equilibrium prices, i.e., for prices that clear the market. Consider a pure exchange economy and assume that there are L goods and I consumers. Consumer i has an endowment $w_i = (w_{i1}, \ldots, w_{iL})$, which she sells at the market at price p and obtains wealth $w_i = p \cdot w_i$. (Here w_i is a vector in R^L). We will assume that endowments are strictly positive, so that each consumer always has positive wealth. Then the consumer buys goods for her consumption at the same price (she may buy back some of the goods she sold). The Marshallian demand of a consumer with wealth w_i is $x_i(p, w_i)$. Define the excess demand vector by:

$$z(p) = \sum_{i=1}^{I} (x_i(p, p \cdot w_i) - w_i).$$

A vector $p \in R^L$ is said to clear the market if,

$$z(p) = 0.$$

Assume there are three goods in economy: apples (good one), oranges (good two), and money and normalize the price of money to be one. Let p be the price of oranges and q is the price of apples and assume that,

$$z_1(p, q) = p^2 - q - 2,$$
$$z_2(p, q) = q - p.$$

Then the equilibrium can be found from the following system:

$$\begin{cases} p^2 - q - 2 = 0, \\ q - p = 0. \end{cases}$$

Since the system is not linear, Cramer's rule cannot be used to solve it. However, the method of consecutive elimination still works. From the second equation: $q = p$ and the first equation becomes,

$$p^2 - p - 2 = 0.$$

It is a quadratic equation, which has two solutions

$$p_1 = 2 \text{ and } p_2 = -1.$$

Obviously, only the positive solution makes any economic sense, therefore $p = q = 2$.

13.5 Problems

(1) Give an example of 2×2 matrices A and B such that,

$$A * B \neq B * A.$$

(2)

Let

$$A = \begin{matrix} 2 & 4 \\ -5 & 3 \end{matrix}$$

and,

$$B = \begin{matrix} 0 & 3 \\ 3 & -2 \end{matrix}$$

Find

(i) $A + B$,
(ii) $2A - B$,
(iii) AB,
(iv) BA.

(3) Find the determinant of a 3×3 matrix A:

$$\begin{matrix} a_{11} & a_{12} & a_{12} \\ a_{21} & a_{22} & a_{23} \\ a_{31} & a_{32} & a_{33} \end{matrix}$$

(4) Use Cramer's rule to find the values of x and y that solve the following two equations simultaneously.

$$\begin{cases} 3x - 2y = 11, \\ 2x + y = 12. \end{cases}$$

Chapter 14

Basics of Calculus

In this chapter, I will introduce the basic technique of calculus, theory of differentiation, integration, and unconstrained maximization. I will also present some fixed point theorems and the Berge maximum theorem and consider such economic applications as theory of the firm, consumer theory, and game theory. I will start with describing some simple sets of real numbers.

14.1 Open and closed sets

The material of this section is covered in Sections 1.3 and 1.4 and of the following several section in Chapter 2 of the main text.

Two classes of sets will play important role in the future: open sets, i.e., sets that contain with each point its neighborhood and their complements, known as closed sets. Suppose the universe of discourse is the real line. Then the following set $(a, b) = \{x : a < x < b\}$ is open, set $[a, b] = \{x : a \leq x \leq b\}$ is closed and sets $[a, b) = \{x : a \leq x < b\}$ and $(a, b] = \{x : a < x \leq b\}$ are neither (i.e., a set need not be either open or closed, moreover R itself is both open and closed). In general:

Definition 1. A set $X \subset R^n$ is called open if for any $a \in X$, there exists $\varepsilon > 0$ such that any x that lies within ε of a belongs to X, where the distance between two points $(x_1, \ldots, x_n)$ and $(y_1, \ldots, y_n)$ is the Euclidean distance given by:

$$d(x, y) = \sqrt{\sum_{i=1}^{n}(x_i - y_i)^2}.$$

Definition 2. A set $F \subset R^n$ is called closed if its complement (set of points not in F) is open.

The interior of set X is the largest open set contained in it, i.e., $A = \text{Int}(X)$ if A is open, $A \subset X$ and for any open B such that $B \subset X$ it is true that $B \subset A$. The closure of F is the smallest closed set that contains F, i.e., $C = \text{cl}(F)$ if C is closed, $F \subset C$ and for any closed D such that $F \subset D$ it is true that $C \subset D$.

Apart from open and closed sets, there exists another class of sets that plays an important role in economics is the class of convex sets. A set is called convex if with any two points it contains the segment that connects them. Formally,

Definition 3. A set $X \subset R^n$ is called convex if for $\forall x_1, x_2 \in X$ and $\forall t \in [0, 1]$ point $x = tx_1 + (1 - t)x_2 \in X$.

14.2 Continuous functions and compact sets

A function is a rule that associates with every point in some set, a single point in another set. Intuitively, it reflects some relations between variables. Functions can be represented by formulas, graphs, tables, and other means. Generally, functions need not have any good properties and can oscillate wildly. An example of such a function is a Dirichlet function, $D(x)$, which is zero at all rational points and one at the irrational ones. However, most function that arise at applications in social and natural sciences behave much better. An important property of a function is continuity.

A function of a single variable is continuous if its graph has no "jumps," so that it can be drawn without lifting pen from paper. In more precise terms, a function $f(\cdot)$ is continuous at point a if we can ensure that the value $f(x)$ of the function is as close as we wish to $f(a)$ by choosing x close enough to a. Here is a completely precise definition for a function of many variables. Recall that, the distance between two points $(x_1, \ldots, x_n)$ and $(y_1, \ldots, y_n)$ is the Euclidean distance given by:

$$d(x, y) = \sqrt{\sum_{i=1}^{n} (x_i - y_i)^2}.$$

Definition 4. Let $f(\cdot) : R^n \to R^m$ be a function. Then $f(\cdot)$ is continuous at $a \in R^n$ if, for any number $\varepsilon > 0$, there is a number $\delta > 0$ such that,

$$d(f(x), f(a)) < \varepsilon, \quad \forall x \in R^n \text{ such that } d(x, a) < \delta.$$

The following result is useful in determining whether a function is continuous.

Theorem 5. *If the functions* f *and* g *are continuous at* x, *then the functions* h *defined by:*

1. $h(x) = f(x) + g(x),$
2. $h(x) = f(x)g(x),$
3. $h(x) = f(x)/g(x), \text{ provided } g(x) \neq 0,$

are continuous at x.

We will call a set $X \subset R^n$ bounded if it can be placed within a ball of finite radius. A closed bounded set is called *compact*.

Theorem 6. *Let* $f : K \to R$ *be continuous and* K *be compact. Then* $f(\cdot)$ *achieves its maximum and its minimum on* K.

14.3 Derivatives and differentiability

Let $X \subset R^n$ and $f : X \to R$.

Definition 7. It is said that,

$$\lim_{x \to a} f(x) = A,$$

if

$$\forall \varepsilon > 0 \ \exists \delta > 0 \ \forall x \in ((x - \delta, x + \delta) \cap X)/\{a\} \ |f(x) - A| < \varepsilon.$$

In the light of this definition, the definition of continuity can be rephrased in the following way: $f(x)$ is continuous at point a iff,

$$\lim_{x \to a} f(x) = f(a).$$

Definition 8. A norm of vector $a \in R^n$ is defined by

$$\|a\| = \sqrt{(a, a)} = \sqrt{\sum_{i=1}^{n} a_i^2}.$$

Definition 9. A function $\alpha(x) : R^n \to R$ is called $o(x)$ (read small o of x) if

$$\lim_{x \to 0} \frac{\alpha(x)}{\|x\|} = 0.$$

Definition 10. A function $f : X \to R$ is said to be differentiable at $x_0 \in \mathrm{Int}(X)$ if there exists a neighborhood V of x and a vector $a \in R^n$ such that for any $h \in R^n : x_0 + h \in V$,

$$f(x_0 + h) - f(x_0) = a \cdot h + o(\|x\|).$$

Definition 11. Let $X \subset R^n$, $f : X \to R$ and $x_0 \in \mathrm{Int}(X)$. The following limit (if it exists),

$$\lim \frac{f(x_{01}, \dots, x_{0i} + h, \dots, x_{0n}) - f(x_0)}{h},$$

is called a partial derivative of f with respect to x_i at point x_0 and denoted $\partial f / \partial x_i(x_0)$. If $n = 1$, then it is called simply a derivative.

Theorem 12. *If $n = 1$, then f is differentiable at x_0 if and only if it has a derivative at x_0.*

If $n > 1$ and function is differentiable, it possesses all the partial derivatives. Reverse, however, is not true. If we assume that function not only possesses all the partial derivatives at x_0 but also that they are continuous at x_0, then it will be differentiable at x_0. The main application of the derivatives is the theory of unconstraint optimization.

Definition 13. Let $f : X \to R$. A point x^* is called local maximum (minimum) of function $f(x)$ if there exists a neighborhood V of x^* if $\forall y \in V$ $f(y) \le f(x^*)$ $(f(y) \ge f(x^*))$.

Maxima and minima of a function are called its extrema.

Theorem 14. *Let $f : X \to R$, $X \subset R^n$ and let it be differentiable. Assume also that $x^* \in \mathrm{Int}X$. Then if x^* is a local extremum, then $\partial f / \partial x_i(x^*) = 0$.*

Reverse is not true, take for example, $f(x) = x^3$. Then $f'(0) = 0$ but it is not an extremum. Note that if $f'(x) < 0$, then f is decreasing at x and if $f'(x) > 0$, it is increasing at x.

14.4 Calculating derivatives

The derivatives of the elementary functions can be calculated from the definition.

Example 15. Let $f(x) = x^2$, then

$$f'(x) = \lim_{\Delta x \to 0} \frac{(x + \Delta x)^2 - x^2}{\Delta x} = \lim_{\Delta x \to 0} (2x + \Delta x) = 2x.$$

In calculating derivatives of more complicated expressions, it is useful to use the following rules:

$$(f(x) + g(x))' = f'(x) + g'(x),$$
$$(cf(x))' = cf'(x),$$
$$[f(x)g(x)]' = f'(x)g(x) + fg'(x),$$
$$\left[\frac{f(x)}{g(x)}\right]' = \frac{f'(x)g(x) - g'(x)f(x)}{g^2(x)},$$
$$[f(g(x))]' = f'(g(x))g'(x),$$
$$\frac{\partial}{\partial y_i} f(z(y)) = \sum_{j=1}^{n} \frac{\partial f}{\partial z_j} \frac{\partial z_j}{\partial y_i}.$$

Here is the list of the derivatives of the most commonly used functions:

$$(x^\beta)' = \beta x^{\beta - 1},$$
$$(e^x)' = e^x,$$
$$\ln' x = \frac{1}{x},$$
$$(a^x)' = a^x \ln a,$$
$$\sin' x = \cos x,$$
$$\cos' x = -\sin x,$$
$$\tan' x = \frac{1}{\cos^2 x},$$

$$\arctan' x = \frac{1}{1+x^2},$$

$$\arcsin' x = \frac{1}{\sqrt{1-x^2}}.$$

14.5 The antiderivative and integral

Definition 16. A function $F(x)$ is called antiderivative (indefinite integral) for $f(x)$ is $F'(x) = f(x)$. If $F(x)$ is antiderivative for $f(x)$ so is $F(x) + C$. We write

$$\int f(x)dx = F(x) + C.$$

Reverting the table of derivatives

$$\int x^\beta dx = \frac{x^{\beta+1}}{\beta+1} + C, \ \beta \neq -1,$$

$$\int e^x dx = e^x + C,$$

$$\int \frac{dx}{x} = \ln x + C,$$

$$\int a^x dx = \frac{a^x}{\ln a} + C, \ a \neq 1,$$

$$\int \sin x dx = -\cos x + C,$$

$$\int \cos x dx = \sin x + C,$$

$$\int \frac{dx}{\cos^2 x} = \tan x + C,$$

$$\int \frac{dx}{1+x^2} = arctgx + C,$$

$$\int \frac{dx}{\sqrt{1-x^2}} = \arcsin x + C.$$

Let $f : [a, b] \to R$ and let $a = x_0 < x_1 < \cdots < x_n = b$. Define

$$\lambda = \max_i |x_i - x_{i-1}|.$$

Let $\xi_i \in (x_{i-1}, x_i)$ and consider a sum,

$$\sum_{i=1}^{n} f(\xi_i)(x_i - x_{i-1}).$$

Assume that as $\lambda \to 0$ this sum goes to some limit, which does not depend on the choice of x_is and ξ_is. Then the function is called Riemann integrable and the value of this limit is denoted by

$$\int_a^b f(x)dx.$$

It can be proved that any continuous function is Riemann integrable. Let $f(x)$ be continuous. Define,

$$F(x) = \int_a^x f(y)dy.$$

Then $F(x)$ is differentiable and $F'(x) = f(x)$. An immediate corollary is the following theorem:

Theorem 17 (Newton–Leibnitz). *Let $F(x)$ be an antiderivative of $f(x)$. Then*

$$\int_a^b f(x)dx = F(b) - F(a).$$

Theorem 18 (Integration by Parts).

$$\int u(x)v'(x)dx = u(x)v(x) - \int u'(x)v(x)dx.$$

Let us use this formula to compute

$$\int x \ln x dx. \tag{14.1}$$

Using Theorem (18) with,

$$f(x) = \ln x, g(x) = x^2/2. \tag{14.2}$$

Then $g'(x) = x$, and (14.1) has a form

$$\int f(x)g'(x)dx, \tag{14.3}$$

where $f(\cdot)$ and $g(\cdot)$ are given by (14.2). Using Theorem (18)

$$\int x \ln x dx = \frac{x^2}{2} \ln x - \int \frac{x^2}{2} \ln' x dx. \qquad (14.4)$$

Using expressions for derivatives and anti-derivatives, provided on pages 171 and 172

$$\int \frac{x^2}{2} \ln' x dx = \int \frac{x}{2} dx = \frac{x^2}{4} + C. \qquad (14.5)$$

Finally,

$$\int x \ln x dx = \frac{x^2}{2} \ln x - \frac{x^2}{4} + C. \qquad (14.6)$$

Integration by parts substantially extends a class of functions for which one can explicitly find the indefinite integral. Consider, however, the following integral:

$$\int x e^{x^2} dx. \qquad (14.7)$$

The integrand cannot be written as sum of the elementary functions multiplied by constants. Though one can perform integration by parts to obtain

$$\int x e^{x^2} dx = \frac{x^2}{2} e^{x^2} - \int x^3 e^{x^2} dx, \qquad (14.8)$$

it does not help in finding the indefinite integral. We need fresh ideas.

One such idea is substitution. Consider an integral

$$\int f(t(x)) t'(x) dx \qquad (14.9)$$

and let $F(\cdot)$ be an anti-derivative of f.

Recall the chain rule

$$[F(t(x))]' = F'(t(x)) t'(x) = f(t(x)) t'(x). \qquad (14.10)$$

Integrating both parts, we obtain

$$F(t(x)) = \int f(t(x)) t'(x) dx = \int f(t) dt. \qquad (14.11)$$

Let us return to (14.7) and write,

$$t(x) = x^2. \tag{14.12}$$

Note that

$$t'(x) = 2x, dt = 2xdx, \tag{14.13}$$

therefore,

$$\int xe^{x^2} dx = \frac{1}{2}\int e^t dt = \frac{e^t}{2} + C = \frac{e^{x^2}}{2} + C. \tag{14.14}$$

The trick in computing an integral is to use the rules of integration such as the ones provided by Theorem (18) and Eq. (14.11), integration techniques such as substitution and integration by parts, and algebraic manipulations of the integrand to reduce it to functions whose anti-derivative is known, either because it is an elementary function or because it has already been evaluated. We will see some more examples in the subsection on definite integrals. Not all anti-derivatives of combinations of elementary functions can be expressed as elementary functions. For example, the anti-derivative of e^{x^2} cannot be expressed using elementary functions. If such anti-derivative is important in applications, a new special function is introduced and its values are tabulated. For example, special function erf($\cdot$) plays an important role in statistics and allows one to evaluate the following integral:

$$\frac{2}{\sqrt{\pi}}\int e^{-x^2} dx = \mathrm{erf}(x) + C. \tag{14.15}$$

14.6 L'Hopital rule

Let $f, g : R \to R.$ be differentiable functions such that $f(a) = g(a) = 0$ and $g'(a) \neq 0$, then

$$\lim_{x \to a} \frac{f(x)}{g(x)} = \frac{f'(a)}{g'(a)}.$$

Example 19. Let us use the l'Hopital Rule to calculate the following limit:

$$\lim_{x \to 0} \frac{\sin x}{x}.$$

In this case $f(x) = \sin x$, $g(x) = x$, therefore $f(0) = g(0) = 0$. Using the table of derivatives of the elementary functions, $f'(x) = \cos x$, $g'(x) = 1 \neq 0$.

Therefore,

$$\lim_{x \to 0} \frac{\sin x}{x} = 1.$$

14.7 Second derivatives and local extrema

Let $f : R \to R$. is a differentiable function. If its derivative is also differentiable, the function f is called twice differentiable and $(f'(x))' = f''(x)$ is called the second derivative of function f. Derivatives of order m are defined in a similar way. L'Hopital rule can be generalized. Let $f, g \in C^n(R)$,

$$f(a) = f'(a) = \cdots = f^{(n)}(a) = g(a) = g'(a) = \cdots g^{(n-1)}(a) = 0,$$
$$g^{(n)}(a) \neq 0.$$

Then,

$$\lim_{x \to a} \frac{f(x)}{g(x)} = \frac{f^{(n)}(a)}{g^{(n)}(a)}.$$

Assume that f is twice differentiable at a and define

$$g(x) = \frac{f(x) - f(a) - f'(x)(x - a)}{x - a}.$$

The above formula defines $g(\cdot)$ at all points except for $x = a$. We will define $g(a)$ in such a way that $g(x)$ will be a continuous function over all R, i.e.,

$$g(a) = \lim_{x \to a} g(x) = 0.$$

Let us calculate $g'(a)$

$$g'(a) = \lim_{x \to a} \frac{g(x) - g(a)}{x - a} = \lim_{x \to a} \frac{f(x) - f(a) - f'(x)(x - a)}{(x - a)^2} = -\frac{f''(a)}{2}.$$

Now, since $g(\cdot)$ is differentiable at a:

$$g(x) - g(a) = g'(a)(x - a) + o(x - a).$$

Taking into account definition of g, facts that $g(a) = 0$, $g'(a) = -f''(a)/2$ and $(x - a)o(x - a) = o([x - a]^2)$ we can write,

$$f(x) - f(a) - f'(x)(x - a) = -\frac{f''(a)}{2}(x - a)^2 + o([x - a]^2).$$

Finally, writing

$$f'(x) = f'(a) + f''(a)(x - a) + o(x - a)$$

and using $(x - a)o(x - a) = o([x - a]^2)$ and $o([x - a]^2) + o([x - a]^2) = o$
$([x - a]^2)$ we get,

$$f(x) - f(a) = f'(a)(x - a) + \frac{f''(a)}{2}(x - a)^2 + o([x - a]^2).$$

This formula implies that if a is a local maximum (minimum), then $f''(a) \leq$
$0 \ (\geq 0)$. Moreover, if $f'(a) = 0$ and $f''(a) > 0 \ (< 0)$, then a is a local
minimum (maximum).

Definition 20. Let $X \subset R^n$ be a convex set. A function $f : X \to R$ is
called convex (concave) if $\forall t \in [0, 1]$ and $\forall x_1, x_2 \in X$,

$$f(tx_1 + (1 - t)x_2) \leq (\geq)tf(x_1) + (1 - t)f(x_2).$$

Assume that f is twice continuously differentiable at a. Fix any $x \in R$
and $t \in [0, 1]$. Let $x_t = tx + (1 - t)a$. Then,

$$f(x_t) - tf(x) - (1 - t)f(a) = t(f(x_t) - f(x)) + (1 - t)(f(x_t) - f(a)).$$

Since,

$$f(x_t) - f(a) = f'(a)(x - a)t + \frac{1}{2}f''(a)(x - a)^2t^2 + o([x - a]^2),$$

$$f(x_t) - f(x) = f'(x)(x - a)(t - 1) + \frac{1}{2}f''(x)(x - a)^2(t - 1)^2 + o([x - a]^2).$$

we get,

$$\lim_{x \to a} \frac{f(x_t) - tf(x) - (1 - t)f(a)}{(x - a)^2} = -\frac{1}{2}f''(a).$$

Function $f(x)$ is convex (concave) iff $\forall x$:

$$f''(x) \geq (\leq)0.$$

Note that it means that the derivative can be zero either only in one point
or on a segment $[a, b]$. Since it changes sign from minus to plus, this point
(points) correspond to local minima if f is convex (maxima if it is convex).
In fact, they determine global minima (maxima).

If for any $t \in (0,1)$

$$f(x_t) > (<)t f(x) - (1-t)f(a),$$

f is called strictly concave (convex).

Proposition 21. *If function is strictly concave (convex) on a convex set X than the global maximum (if it exists) is unique.*

Proof. Suppose f achieves its maximum at two different points x_1 and x_2, that is

$$f(x_1) = f(x_2) = M \geq f(x), \tag{14.16}$$

for any $x \in X$. Since X is convex

$$\frac{x_1 + x_2}{2} \in X.$$

By strict concavity of $f(\cdot)$

$$f\left(\frac{x_1 + x_2}{2}\right) > \frac{1}{2}f(x_1) + \frac{1}{2}f(x_2) = M,$$

which contradicts (14.16). □

Note that here we used proof by contradiction. We had to prove that statement $A : f(x_1) = f(x_2) \geq f(x) \; \forall x \in X$ implied statement $B : x_1 = x_2$. Instead, we proved that statement $not\,B : x_1 \neq x_2$ implies $not\,A : \exists x \in X : f(x) > f(x_1) = f(x_2)$.

Definition 22. A function $f : R^n \to R$ is called quasiconcave if $\{x \in R^n : f(x) \geq c\}$ is convex for any c.

Definition 23. It is easy to see that $f(x)$ is quasiconcave if $\forall t \in [0,1]$

$$f(tx_1 + (1-t)x_2) \geq \min(f(x_1), f(x_2)).$$

A function $f : R^n \to R$ is called quasiconvex if $\{x \in R^n : f(x) \leq c\}$ is convex for any c.

It is easy to see that $f(x)$ is quasiconvex if $\forall t \in [0,1]$

$$f(tx_1 + (1-t)x_2) \leq \max(f(x_1), f(x_2)).$$

If the inequalities are strict for all $t \in (0,1)$, the function is called strictly quasiconcave (quasiconvex).

14.7.1 *More matrix algebra*

To proceed further, we need some more facts from matrix algebra.

Definition 24. A square matrix A is symmetric if $a_{ij} = a_{ji}$.

Definition 25. Symmetric matrix A is negatively (positively) semidefinite if $\forall x \in R^n$:

$$(x, Ax) \leq (\geq)0.$$

If the inequality is strict for $x \neq 0$, then A is called negatively (positively) definite.

Let $f:$ be twice continuously differentiable function. Construct a matrix $D(a)$ where,

$$d_{ij} = \frac{\partial^2 f}{\partial x_i \partial x_j}(a).$$

It can be proved that this matrix is symmetric (Young's theorem).

A twice differentiable function f is convex (concave) in a neighborhood of point a iff $D(a)$ is positively (negatively) semidefinite. For a proof consider

$$h(t) = f(a + tx).$$

Similarly, if a is a local maximum (minimum) of f then $D(a)$ is negatively (positively) semidefinite. If it is positively (negatively) definite and $\nabla f(a) = 0$, then a is a local minimum (maximum).

For $n \times n$ matrix A define $A_1 = a_{11}$, $A_2 = \begin{smallmatrix} a_{11} & a_{12} \\ a_{21} & a_{22} \end{smallmatrix}$, etc. Then matrix A is positively semidefinite (negatively semidefinite) if $\det A_i \geq 0$ $((-1)^i \det A_i \geq 0)$. If all inequalities are strict, the matrix is positively definite (negatively definite).

A complex number λ is called an eigenvalue of matrix A if $\det(A - \lambda I) = 0$, where I is a matrix with 1s on the main diagonal and zeros elsewhere. If A is symmetric and real all its eigenvalues are real. A matrix is positively semidefinite (positively definite, negatively semidefinite, negatively definite) if all its eigenvalues are non-negative (positive, non-positive, negative).

14.8 Envelope theorem for unconstraint optimization

The envelope theorem answers the question: how the value function changes in response to small changes in the parameters.

Theorem 26. *Let $f(x, y)$ be differentiable and $x \in X \subset R^n$, where $X-$ is compact. Define*

$$V(y) = \max_{x \in X} f(x, y),$$

and assume that maximum $x(y)$ is achieved in the interior of X. Then

$$V'(y) = \frac{\partial f(x(y), y)}{\partial y}.$$

14.9 Continuous random variables

Let θ be a random variable that can take any values in the segment $[a, b]$. The cumulative distribution function of θ is defined as

$$F_\theta(x) = \Pr(\theta < x).$$

It is easy to see that $F_\theta(x)$ is weakly increasing and

$$F_\theta(a) = 0, \ F_\theta(b) = 1.$$

Now,

$$\Pr(x \leq \theta < x + \varepsilon) = F_\theta(x + \varepsilon) - F_\theta(x) \approx F_\theta'(x)\varepsilon.$$

As $\varepsilon \to 0$, the above equality becomes precise, i.e.,

$$\lim_{\varepsilon \to 0} \frac{\Pr(x \leq \theta < x + \varepsilon)}{\varepsilon} = F_\theta'(x) = f_\theta(x),$$

where $f_\theta(x)$ is called a probability density function (p.d.f.) of θ.

Proposition 27. *For any random variable θ distributed on $[a, b]$ its pdf (if it exists) has the following properties:*

1. $f_\theta(x) \geq 0$ *for* $\forall x \in [a, b]$,

2.

$$\int_a^x f_\theta(x)dx = F_\theta(x)$$

$\forall x \in [a, b]$. *In particular,*

$$\int_a^b f_\theta(x)dx = 1.$$

The reverse is also true. Any function $f : [a, b] \to R$ such that $f(x) \geq 0$ for $\forall x \in [a, b]$ and

$$\int_a^b f(x)dx = 1$$

defines some random variable on $[a, b]$.

14.10 Correspondences

Recall that a correspondence as a rule that takes elements of set X into subsets of Y. We want to generalize notion of continuity for the correspondences. We will always assume that the image set Y is compact.

Definition 28. A correspondence $f : X \to Y$ is called upper-hemicontinuous (u.h.c.) if for any $(x_n, y_n) \to (x, y)$ $[y_n \in f(x_n) \; \forall n] \Rightarrow [y \in f(x)]$.

This definition says that a correspondence is u.h.c when its graph is closed. If correspondence f is u.h.c. and single-valued, i.e., $f(\cdot)$ is a function, then this function is continuous.

Definition 29. A correspondence $f : X \to Y$ is called convex (non-empty, compact) valued if for any $x \in X$ the set $f(x)$ is convex, non-empty, compact.

The two basic fixed point theorems are

Theorem 30 (Kakutani). *Let $f : X \to X$ be a non-empty and convex valued, u.h.c. correspondence and X be a convex, compact set. Then there exists $x^* \in X : x^* \in f(x^*)$.*

Theorem 31 (Brower). *Let $f : X \to X$ be a continuous function and X be a convex, compact set. Then there exists $x^* \in X : x^* = f(x^*)$.*

The main application of the fixed point theorems in economics is proving the existence of competitive equilibrium and the existence of Nash equilibrium and some forms of its refinements in games. For this purpose, it is important to figure out the conditions that guarantee that the correspondences that maps parameters of a maximization problem into the set of the maximizers is u.h.c. For this purpose, we need the Berge Maximum Theorem.

Definition 32. A correspondence $f : X \rightarrow Y$ is called lower-hemicontinuous (l.h.c.) if for any $\{x_n\}_{n=0}^{\infty} : x_n \in X$ for $\forall n \in N$ and $x_n \rightarrow x \in X$, and any $y \in f(x)$ there exists a sequence $\{y_n\}_{n=0}^{\infty}$ such that $y_n \rightarrow y$ and $y_n \in f(x_n)$.

Intuitively, this definition says that the graph of the correspondence cannot suddenly become "fatter."

Definition 33. A correspondence $f : X \rightarrow Y$ is called continuous if it is both l.h.c. and u.h.c.

Theorem 34 (Berge Maximum Theorem). *Let $X \subset R^n$ be a compact set, $u(\cdot, \cdot) : X \times Y \rightarrow R$ is a continuous function and $\Gamma : Y \rightarrow X$ is a continuous correspondence and for $\forall y \in Y$ the set $\Gamma(y) \neq \varnothing$ is compact. Define value function $v(\cdot) : Y \rightarrow R$ and maximizer correspondence $\phi(\cdot) : Y \rightarrow X$ by:*

$$v(y) = \max u(x, y)$$
$$s.t. \ x \in \Gamma(y),$$

$$\phi(y) = \arg\max u(x, y)$$
$$s.t. \ x \in \Gamma(y).$$

Then $v(\cdot)$ is continuous and $\phi(y) \neq \varnothing$ for $\forall y \in Y$ and u.h.c.

Proof. First, note that since $\Gamma(y) \neq \varnothing$ is compact and $u(\cdot, y)$ is continuous, $\phi(y) \neq \varnothing$ for $\forall y \in Y$. To prove that $\phi(\cdot)$ is u.h.c. consider a sequence $(x_n, y_n) \rightarrow (x, y)$ such that $x_n \in \phi(y_n)$. We have to prove that $x \in \phi(y)$. Assume, to the contrary that $x \notin \phi(y)$. Note that since $\Gamma(\cdot)$ is u.h.c. $x \in \Gamma(y)$, hence $\exists x' \in \Gamma(y)$ such that

$$u(x', y) > u(x, y). \tag{14.17}$$

Since $\Gamma(\cdot)$ is l.h.c. there exists a sequence $\{x_n''\}_{n=0}^{\infty}$ such that $x_n'' \in \Gamma(y_n)$ and $x_n'' \rightarrow x'$. Since $x_n \in \phi(y_n)$, this implies that $u(x_n'', y_n) \leq u(x_n, y_n)$. Passing to the limit and taking into account continuity of $u(\cdot, \cdot)$, this implies $u(x', y) \leq u(x, y)$ in contradiction with (14.17). Now let $y_n \rightarrow y$. Since

$\phi(y_n) \neq \varnothing$ for $\forall n \in N$ $\exists x_n \in \phi(y_n)$. Since X is compact, there exists a subsequence of $\{x_n\}$ that is converging to $x \in X$. To simplify notations w.l.o.g. assume that $x_n \to x$. Since ϕ is u.h.c. $x \in \phi(y)$.

$$\lim_{n \to \infty} v(y_n) = \lim_{n \to \infty} u(x_n, y_n) = u(x, y) = v(y). \qquad (14.18)$$

The first equality follows from the fact that $x_n \in \phi(y_n)$, the second from $x_n \to x$, $y_n \to y$ and continuity of u, and the third from $x \in \phi(y)$. $\qquad \square$

14.11 Problems

(1) Assume $f \in C^n(R)$. Use induction to prove that,

$$f(x) = \sum_{k=0}^{n} \frac{f^{(k)}(a)}{k!}(x-a)^k + o([x-a]^n),$$

here $n! = 1 * 2 * \cdots * n$, $0! = 1$.

(2) Prove that,

$$o(x) + o(x) = o(x),$$
$$o(tx) = o(x).$$

Index

Printed in the United States
By Bookmasters